STONEWORK of the MAYA

Edward Ranney

STONEWORK of the MAYA

UNIVERSITY OF NEW MEXICO PRESS

Albuquerque

Designed by Dan Stouffer

First edition

Reprinted 1974

Composed by the University of New Mexico Printing Plant
Printed by The Meriden Gravure Company
Bound by The C. J. Krehbiel Company

*Affectionately and gratefully
dedicated to my parents, Mr. and
Mrs. George A. Ranney, and to
the memory of my grandparents,
Mr. and Mrs. Edward L. Ryerson*

Archaeological studies and the history of science are concerned with things only as technical products, while art history has been reduced to a discussion of the meaning of things without much attention to their technical and formal organization. The task of the present generation is to construct a history of things that will do justice both to meaning and being, both to the scheme and to the thing. This purpose raises the familiar existential dilemma between meaning and being. We are discovering little by little all over again that what a thing means is not more important than what it is; that expression and form are equivalent challenges to the historian; and that to neglect either meaning or being, either essence or existence, deforms our comprehension of both.

George Kubler
The Shape of Time

Preface

In early 1970, I photographed at a number of archaeological sites in southern Mexico. At that time I had no intention of undertaking an extensive photographic study of Maya monuments. Rather, my aim was to visit a number of pre-Hispanic sites in order to gain a broader perspective on the different traditions of stonework throughout ancient America. My main concern was to return to a long-range photographic exploration of the landscape and stonework of the Incas, in southern Peru.

Nevertheless, my experience at Palenque and other Maya sites awakened a strong personal desire to photograph much more extensively throughout the Maya lowlands. By the time I was able to return to the area in late 1970, I had not only become involved in a project of considerable scope but was also convinced of the need for two comparative studies of ancient American stonework—one focusing exclusively on the Maya, the other on the Inca.

Although the stonework of the Maya is representative of very specific traditions of architecture and sculpture, my intention has not been to provide scientific documentation of the architecture and sculpture or to present only the most important or best-known monuments. Rather, I have photographed the architecture and sculpture as part of the natural setting in which they stand today. In this sense, *Stonework of the Maya* is a study of the interdependence of the cultural and natural landscapes of the ancient Maya.

Each of the sites represented in this study is characterized by a distinct and unique sense of place as well as by strong individual traditions. The stonework of the architecture and sculpture is the most enduring expression of these traditions, and by nature it is both specific and metaphoric, both a world unto itself and an elusive echo of the past.

Archaeological research continually provides us with critical new insights into various aspects of this stonework. The monumental sculpture, for example, has increasingly been shown to record and depict actual personal histories of the Maya elite as well as to bear cyclical calendrical inscriptions. Many major architectural structures have been excavated and reconstructed so that we now have a very immediate, literal vision of how some of the great ceremonial centers once appeared during the Classic Period, roughly A.D. 250–900.

But along with amplifying our factual knowledge of the ancient Maya, we should also be continuously aware of the value and need for purely visual interpretations of the monuments, interpretations which though not always scientifically informative do inform us in other ways, particularly in giving us a feeling for the spirit of the culture. In this sense, a photograph, like an archaeological artifact itself, has the unique potential for providing an intensely evocative expression of an ancient culture. Both a photograph and an artifact are by nature a peculiar mixture of poetry and fact. They can be purely informative and factual, or they can be entirely satisfying within themselves, complete and independent esthetic, emotional wholes. The process of photographing within a cultural landscape as specific as that of the ancient Maya obviously brings us face to face with subjects that demand to be seen as things in themselves. The photographs that result, like the monuments themselves, please us according to our own prejudices, according to what we expect of a photograph and what we think it can or should do.

In photographing the Maya landscape, I have been guided by forces other than reason and knowledge. The archaeological facts presented in this study are more the result of a very personal need to know certain specific things than they are an expression of a systematic, professional knowledge of an ancient culture. More simply, the photographs themselves came first, and have been the motivating force and focus. In this sense, they, like the monuments which they present, both constitute a world within themselves and exist as metaphors of a universe far more vast and complex than any one literal image or any single archaeological artifact.

The ancient Maya believed that the natural elements and forces have their own undeniable logic, their own divine reasons for being. The monuments were created to give symbolic expression to these animistic, divine forces as well as to define and glorify man's relationship to the gods. It is hard for us today fully to understand the combined utilitarian and spiritual purposes of these monuments—although not too distant in our own past are the great Gothic cathedrals, our expression of a common spiritual need.

Our feelings when we visit a Maya site depend largely upon our personal approach to the past, upon our willingness to enter a spiritual as well as a physical landscape. Whether reconstructed or in ruins, the stonework continues to embody the enduring presence of a people and their gods—the living substance of a world that is not so distant or remote from us as it may seem.

A number of persons and institutions have had an active part in helping me to bring this project to completion, and to them I extend my thanks. I am particularly grateful to Richard Bliss, director of East Hill School, Chester, Vermont, both for the leave of absence during which I was first able to photograph in Mexico and for his continuing personal interest in the study. To the Instituto Nacional de Antropología e Historia of Mexico and to its caretakers throughout Mexico, I extend my gratitude for facilitating my work at the archaeological sites. I owe the opportunity for successful work at Yaxchilán and Bonampak to Gertrude Duby Blom, and I am especially grateful to her for permission to translate and quote from Frans Blom's unpublished article, "Yaxchilán, la ciudad maravillosa de los mayas."

Hugh Edwards and Marie Czach, both former curators of photography at the Art Institute of Chicago, provided important early encouragement to expand the initial photographs into book form; Arthur Bullowa and Michael Hoffman of Aperture, Inc. have been equally encouraging and helpful. Other photographers have also been helpful, particularly in giving me a sense of participation in enduring, common concerns far beyond the scope of one person alone. In this sense, Paul Caponigro and William Clift have given especially thoughtful, timely suggestions. Richard Faller, Ross Harris, Laura Gilpin, Arthur LaZar, David Plowden, and Arthur Siegal have offered valuable personal observations as they saw the work in progress.

I am exceedingly grateful to the librarians of the following institutions for making their resources available to me: Na-Bloom, Centro de Estudios Científicos, San Cristóbal de Las Casas, Chiapas, Mexico; Peabody Museum of Archaeology and Ethnology, Harvard University, Cambridge, Massachusetts; Laboratory of Anthropology and Museum of International Folk Art, both of Santa Fe, New Mexico; University of New Mexico, Albuquerque, New Mexico. I am also grateful to Douglas Schwartz, director of the School of American Research, Santa Fe, for permission to read the seminar papers published as *The Classic Maya Collapse*, edited by T. Patrick Culbert.

A number of persons have made valuable suggestions concerning the preparation of a text for this study. Ian Graham has been especially helpful in providing information on Yaxchilán; Jeremy Sabloff's general comments and encouragement have also been much appreciated. I am particularly grateful to Charles Gallenkamp, author of *Maya*, and to Allen Wardwell, former curator of primitive art at the Art Institute of Chicago, for their careful readings of the original manuscript. Robert Wauchope's critical comments have helped immeasurably to bring the project to its final form. I take full responsibility, however, for any errors of interpretation or historical fact.

On a personal level, I would like to thank Vida Clift for her sensitive reading of the text and my sister, Nancy Ranney Levi, for her perceptive and informative suggestions. My sincere thanks are also extended to Mr. and Mrs. Theodore Dreier for their companionship and hospitality in Mexico and to Mr. and Mrs. Jerome Hunsaker, Jr., for making possible a brief but valuable return to Yucatán in 1972. To my wife Melanie, my deepest gratitude for her unfailing help and involvement throughout the entire project.

Contents

Preface   vii

List of Plates   xii

Map   xvi

    I.   Tikal   1

    II.   Copán   15

    III.   Quiriguá   36

    IV.   Yaxchilán   39

    V.   Bonampak   52

    VI.   Palenque   55

    VII.   Dzibilchaltún   67

    VIII.   Cobá   70

    IX.   The Puuc   72

    X.   Uxmal   80

    XI.   Chichén Itzá   94

    XII.   Tulum   108

Bibliography   115

Index   118

List of Plates

Tikal

1. Temple I is the dominant structure of central Tikal.
2. Temple II faces Temple I across the Great Plaza, with Temple III on the left and Temple IV on the right.
3. Stela 3 is representative of Early classic stelae at Tikal.
4. Tikal's Late Classic stelae have a rounded, tombstone-like shape.
5. Plain stelae and altars were always dedicated before the eastern pyramid of Tikal's Twin-Pyramid Complexes.
6. Stela 22 and Altar 10 stand within an open enclosure at the north end of Twin-Pyramid Complex Q.
7. Only the carving at the base of Stela 21 has survived.
8. Unlike other Late Classic stelae of Tikal, Stela 5 has the hieroglyphic text carved on its sides.
9. The south side of Altar 7 shows the head of the death god resting on a plate.
10. The plain stelae of Twin-Pyramid Complex R stand in a glade essentially as they were found.

Copán

11. Stela 13 and its circular altar stand on an open hillside several miles east of Copán's Acropolis.
12. The Ball Court is prominently located between the Great Plaza on the north and the Court of the Hieroglyphic Stairway on the south.
13. Two open vaults face one another across the Ball Court.
14. The Reviewing Stand is named for the steps and platform, thought to resemble a grandstand.
15. Altar Q is one of two monuments standing in the West Court.
16. The flat stone slab known at Altar T is almost inconspicuous at the west end of the Hieroglyphic Court.
17. The magnificent altar dedicated with Stela D in A.D. 736 represents a striking portrayal of the death god.
18. The majority of Copán's eighth-century stelae and altars are grouped together in the Great Plaza.
19. Slender Stela P, dedicated in A.D. 623, is the only stela in the West Court, and is probably the earliest one on the Copán Acropolis.
20. Stela 5, outside the protected archaeological site of Copán near the road to the village of Copán, was dedicated about A.D. 667.
21. The carving of Stela B is characteristic of the elaborate, deep-relief sculptural style that developed at Copán, early in the eighth century.
22. The back, or west side, of Stela B is decorated with a large stylized face.
23. The delicate carving of the figure on Stela A approaches the full round.
24. The robed figure of Stela H is thought to represent a female member of Copán's elite.
25. The extremely deep ornate relief of Stela N indicates that it is perhaps the latest stela at Copán.
26. The glyphs inscribed on the back of Stela F are carved in groups of four, each group enclosed within a rope loop and surrounded by deep grooves representing feathers.
27. All sides of the inscrutable altar accompanying Stela N are carved with the grotesque limbs and features of an unidentifiable mythological creature.

Quiriguá

28. An early portrayal of the figure known as Ruler I appears on the west side of Stela J.
29. Stela E, thirty-five feet high, is the tallest known stela erected by the Maya.

Yaxchilán

30. The three beautiful doorway lintels of Temple 33 bear inscriptions dating within five years of one another, and indicate the temple was dedicated around A.D. 755.
31. The roof comb of Temple 20 stands almost even with the temple's front wall.
32. Lintel 42 is still in place in Temple 42, high above the Usumacinta River.
33. Lintel 2, of Temple 33, shows Bird Jaguar in A.D. 757 with the five-year-old descendant of Shield Jaguar.

34. In Lintel 3, also still in place in Temple 33, Bird Jaguar stands on the right, facing an important ally.
35. This sculptural fragment is part of Stela 7, which marks the completion of Katun 17 and commemorates the accession of Shield Jaguar's descendant as ruler of Yaxchilán.
36. Lintel 22 is remarkable for its rows of delicately carved small glyphs.
37. Lintel 27 is well concealed by jungle growth. The small glyphs on its east side are barely discernible.
38. Many badly eroded sculptural fragments, such as these identified as possible pieces of Stela 4, lie scattered throughout the unexcavated area of Yaxchilán.

Bonampak

39. Stela 1 dates from the late eighth century and is one of the largest stelae dedicated by the Maya.
40. Stela 2 is one of two stelae set on the stairway leading to the small temples of Bonampak.

Palenque

41. The view from the Temple of the Inscriptions overlooks Palenque's Palace Complex and north group of buildings.
42. The north court, the largest and probably the latest of the Palace courts, was apparently finished during the eighth century.
43. The largest temple at Palenque is the Temple of the Inscriptions.
44. The Temple of the Sun is the best preserved of the three small temples grouped together around a plaza on the eastern side of Palenque.
45. The Temple of the Sun faces directly east across the plaza to the Temple of the Foliated Cross.
46. The wall bordering the west side of the Palace's north court is decorated with a few relief carvings.
47. The oval plaque still in place in a wall of Palace House E portrays a woman offering a crown with headdress to a seated ruler.
48. The roughly carved figures on the eastern side of the Palace's north court are totally unlike the classically conceived figures of the Palace tablets.

Dzibilchaltún

49. The Temple of the Seven Dolls is the most striking of Dzibilchaltún's few remaining structures.

Cobá

50. One of the more distinct remains at the vast, overgrown site of Cobá is the imposing temple-pyramid known as Nohuch-Mul.

The Puuc

51. Unlike other Puuc chambered pyramids, Edzná's dominant structure is built over a smaller temple-pyramid of the Petén type and overlooks a central plaza and compact acropolis.
52. Sayil's imposing Palace is given an expansive openness through the innovative use of cylindrical doorway colums.
53. Set at the foot of the rolling Puuc hills, Labná's ceremonial archway and small temple-pyramid are separated from the Palace building by a vast plaza.
54. A stylized form of the Chac mask is relentlessly repeated on the facade of Kabáh's palace-like structure, the Codz-Poop.
55. Chac masks, detail of the Codz-Poop.

Uxmal

56. The back, or east side, of the Pyramid of the Magician rises to a height of about 125 feet.
57. The main temple of the Pyramid of the Magician is built in the Chenes style, with the temple doorway forming the gaping mouth of a large serpent mask.
58. The main entrance to the large enclosed quadrangle known as the Palomas, or dove, group is located at the center of its northern building.
59. The western side of the Pyramid of the Magician overlooks the asymmetrical Nunnery Quadrangle.
60. The west Nunnery building is considered the latest structure of the Nunnery Quadrangle.
61. The simplicity of the frieze of the east Nunnery building makes it one of the finest examples of Puuc design.
62. The Governor's Palace stands upon a twenty-three-foot artificial platform and faces to the east over a broad open terrace.
63. The twenty-five-foot archways of the Governor's Palace originally served as open passages to either side of the building.
64. The House of the Turtles is finished with a veneer masonry that ranks with the finest examples of Puuc stonework.

Chichén Itzá

65. The massive Nunnery was built with the rough block wall and slab vault masonry techniques inherited from the southern lowlands.
66. The Nunnery Annex is a late addition to the main building.
67. Just a few feet from the Nunnery Annex stands the Iglesia, or church, a thick-walled temple of only one room.
68. The fully reconstructed Temple of the Three Lintels shows both the architectural design and the fine veneer masonry stonework typical of the pure Puuc style.

69. The Caracol is named for the snail-like, spiral form of its interior stairway.
70. The Casa Colorada, or red house, is set upon a platform to the west of the Caracol.
71. The Castillo, dating from the Mexican occupation of Chichén Itzá, was dedicated to the cult of Kukulcán, the deified culture hero of central Mexico whose symbol was the feathered serpent.
72. The upper Temple of the Jaguars stands atop the thirty-foot east wall of the Ball Court.
73. A typical Mexican warrior is depicted on the square portico columns of the upper Temple of the Jaguars.

Tulum

74. The view south along the coast at Tulum shows Structure 45 on the left, the Castillo behind it, standing with its back to the sea, and the diminutive Temple of the Diving God on the right.
75. Still in place above the doorway of the Temple of the Diving God is the peculiar, upside-down stucco figure for which the small temple is named.
76. The Caribbean Sea from the northern end of Tulum.

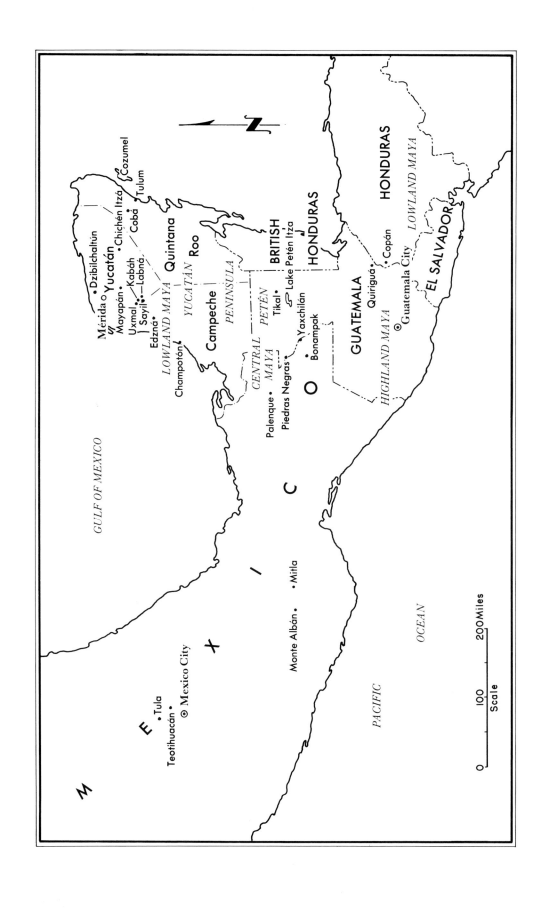

I. Tikal

"Place where spirit voices are heard"

The word *cal* (pronounced with the usual *k*-sound) signifies in the Maya tongue, the throat, the esophagus. When the word becomes *kal, kalil* (pronounced with strongly emphasized *k*-sound), it means voices, calls, cries.

The Mayas believe that at midnight (especially during the great festivals), their ancestors return to earth and, adorned as in the days of their glory, wander about in the forsaken temples and palaces, where their spirit-voices are heard in the air. Therefore all important ruins in this land are regarded as enchanted, *encantadas,* and timid people do not like to sleep alone in their desolate chambers.

> Teobert Maler, 1904
> *Explorations in the Department
> of Petén, Guatemala, 1911*

Tikal is situated deep within the isolated and sparsely inhabited Petén district of northern Guatemala. As a result of a decade of intensive excavation and reconstruction, the site has become one of the most impressive of all Maya centers. An immense body of knowledge concerning the southern lowland Maya has resulted from its excavation. No other southern Maya site offers the visitor such an impressive vista of massive monumental architecture. The sheer scale of its temple-pyramid style and its great size are overwhelming.

Excavation has revealed evidence of permanent settlement at Tikal as early as 600 B.C., one of the earliest known dates for the settlement of the southern lowlands. The natural advantages encouraging settlement of this isolated area are not readily apparent, and why the distinctive elements of Maya civilization first appeared here in the Petén continues to puzzle scholars.

An upland rise of 210 feet dominates the rain forest around Tikal and provides some relief from the swampy *bajos,* or low areas, during the rainy season. Initially the drainage from this hill may have provided a thicker, more fertile topsoil than was found elsewhere, and early settlement and ceremonial activity may have naturally developed on the inviting nearby elevation. One important natural resource found in abundance throughout the area surrounding Tikal is a hard workable flint from which the Maya made tools and religious objects. The flint proved to be an important item of trade for the Petén Maya, in exchange for which they received obsidian and jade from the highlands. The development of an efficient trade system was crucial to the growth of Maya civilization. The inhabitants of the Petén were dependent upon outlying areas not only for objects of wealth but also for such daily necessities as salt and hard stone to serve as *metates,* or grinding stones.

As early as 200 B.C., Tikal is known to have had a large population. Massive temple construction already dominated the North Acropolis. By 100 B.C., the Great Plaza and the North Terrace had become well established. At Tikal the beginning of the Early Classic Period is dated around A.D. 250; the earliest known dated inscription anywhere in the Maya lowlands was dedicated there in A.D. 292.

The intense building activity during the three hundred years of Tikal's Early Classic Period was concentrated mainly on the North Acropolis. This massive ceremonial platform is the result of at least twelve different layers of temple construction. Throughout the Maya area early temples invariably served as foundations or as building material for the construction of later temple-pyramids. Neither a temple nor a tomb of a dignitary sometimes buried beneath it was considered inviolable. The contents of such a tomb were often destroyed, looted, or reburied in a different location. Similarly, many of Tikal's other monuments, particularly stelae, were mutilated, apparently to destroy their symbolic power.

The Late Classic Period of Tikal, A.D. 550–900, saw the construction of the site's five great temple-pyramids, all dedicated between A.D. 700 and A.D. 810. Temple II, the squat temple-pyramid on the west side of the Great Plaza, is known to have been the first constructed, about A.D. 700. Temples I and V were built a few years later. Temple IV, the largest of all Maya temple-pyramids, was dedicated in A.D. 741. Temple III, probably dating from about A.D. 810, reflects the final stage of Tikal's massive architectural style.

The impressive mass and height of the pyramids emphasize the symbolic importance of the small two- or three-room temples perched upon them. By all indications, these temples were the exclusive domain of the priests and rulers. Certainly as usable structures they were little more than shrines or great altars. But since the religious rites of the priests presumably required secrecy and obscurity, the dark, confined spaces of the thick-walled vaults may well have been considered an asset rather than a liability.

The Maya architect was concerned mainly with the design of exterior space. Throughout Tikal's Late Classic Period, particular attention was paid to careful spatial arrangement of increasingly elaborate building complexes. Particularly important were the ceremonial groups known as Twin-Pyramid Complexes. These consisted of

2

truncated pyramids, low buildings, and sculptural monuments, all of which were dedicated together to commemorate the completion of a *katun*—a period of about twenty years. At Tikal, most of the seven of these complexes were joined to the other ceremonial groups by broad elevated causeways.

The Late Classic Period also saw the proliferation of the buildings usually referred to as palaces. These were built around enclosed courtyards, often standing several stories high. They were presumably used only by Tikal's elite for residential and administrative purposes or as centers of religious training. As residences, these palaces would have been the most imposing house structures of Tikal, and would attest to heavily concentrated settlement at the center of the site. The estimated population of Tikal during the Late Classic Period ranges from a conservative ten thousand inhabitants for the 16 square kilometers of Tikal proper to thirty-nine thousand for the 63 square kilometers of the entire central zone. By including the outlying zones, or an overall area of 123 square kilometers, a maximum population of some forty-five thousand is postulated for the site.

Evidence of cultural contact with Teotihuacán, the large urban center of central Mexico, around A.D. 500 may account to some degree for Tikal's increasingly complex development during the Late Classic Period. Even though Tikal never adopted the urban grid and *barrio* settlement pattern used at Teotihuacán, specialized professions and increased economic diversity did characterize the Late Classic culture of Tikal, and an intricate stratified class system replaced the simple chiefdom society that existed at most Maya Ceremonial centers. Religion was traditionally the integrative force of Maya culture, but at Tikal there must have been complex social and administrative problems that could have been handled only by a centralized bureaucracy. Workers in food, trade, and construction, as well as in many specialized areas, had to be properly supervised. Thus, in function as well as in concentration of population, Late Classic Tikal may well have closely resembled a city rather than a traditional Maya ceremonial center.

The nonelite residents of Tikal were apparently considerably affected by the Late Classic development. The traditional clan system of the Maya peasant, based on localized lineages, broke down as Tikal's increasingly complex society emerged. Skeletal remains also give some evidence of chronic food shortages and malnutrition among the lower classes. Certainly population pressure on the land, capably of supporting only limited agriculture, coupled with other stress factors of Late Classic society, must have had much to do with the cultural decline that had set in at Tikal by A.D. 790. By A.D. 830 construction was on the wane, and the end of Classic Period ceremonial life apparently came quickly, with the last known Long Count inscription of Tikal dedicated in A.D. 869.

Although Tikal continued to be inhabited during Postclassic times, perhaps even as late as the fourteenth century, not long after the close of the ninth century its population was reduced by almost ninety percent. Its great cultural traditions became but a dim memory of the past. Tombs were looted, and fragments of Classic Period monuments were awkwardly reset. The Postclassic Period population were apparently determined to maintain a monument cult—they added almost twice as many plain stelae and altars to those already in the Great Plaza. These stand today as mute testimony to the importance of ceremonial activity in itself and as symbols of the survivors' most enduring link with the past. For to them, as J. Eric Thompson suggests, "sacredness lay in the stone itself—folk memory of importance in the past—not in the figures or hieroglyphic texts inscribed upon it."[1]

1. *Handbook of Middle American Indians,* vol. 2 (Austin: University of Texas Press, 1965), p. 347.

1. Temple I is the dominant structure of central Tikal, its ornamental roof comb towering about 145 feet above the Great Plaza. As with other temple-pyramids at this site, an elite burial was made beneath the pyramid before it was built.

2. Temple II faces Temple I across the Great Plaza and stands about 125 feet high. Temple III, on the left, and Temple IV, on the right, are, respectively, 180 and 212 feet high. Tikal's roof combs show traces of having been painted cream, red, green, and blue; the temples may have been entirely red.

3. *Stela 3, dedicated in A.D. 488, is representative of Early Classic stelae at Tikal, which are generally smaller and less symmetrical than Late Classic ones. The inscriptions of Early Classic stelae usually appear on the sides of the monument, the front being unadorned.*

4. Tikal's Late Classic stelae have a rounded, tombstone-like shape and stand from five to eleven feet high. Like the carved monuments, the plain stelae and altars were probably painted red but otherwise were undecorated.

5. Plain stelae and altars were always dedicated before the eastern pyramid of Tikal's Twin-Pyramid Complexes. The nine pairs of monuments associated with the truncated pyramid of Twin-Pyramid Complex Q have been reset before the reconstructed ceremonial platform.

6. *Stela 22 and Altar 10 stand within an open enclosure at the
north end of Twin-Pyramid Complex Q. Both monuments are
carved, the stela inscription providing a dedicatory date of A.D. 771
for the entire ceremonial complex.*

7. *Only the carving at the base of Stela 21 has survived, but the hieroglyphic text is sufficient to provide a dedicatory date of A.D. 736. The accompanying altar, like many others at Tikal, was carved with a bound captive figure.*

8. *Unlike other Late Classic stelae of Tikal, Stela 5 has the hieroglyphic text carved on its sides. These glyphs on the east side are part of an unusually long inscription dating the stela at A.D. 744.*

9. *The south side of Altar 7 shows the head of the death god resting on a plate. The altar was dedicated with Stela 24 at the base of Temple III. The eroded text of the broken stela suggests a date of A.D. 810 for the last of Tikal's great temple-pyramids.*

10. *The plain stelae of Twin-Pyramid Complex R stand in a glade essentially as they were found. Dedicated in A.D. 790, the R Complex is the latest of this kind of ceremonial group at Tikal.*

II. Copán

Of the moral effect of the monuments themselves, standing as they do in the depths of a tropical forest, silent and solemn, strange in design, excellent in sculpture, rich in ornament, different from the works of any other people, their uses and purposes, their whole history so entirely unknown, with hieroglyphics explaining all, but perfectly unintelligible, I shall not pretend to convey any idea. Often the imagination was pained in gazing at them. The tone which pervades the ruins is that of deep solemnity. An imaginative mind might be infected with superstitious feelings. From constantly calling them by that name in our intercourse with the Indians, we regarded these solemn memorials as "idols"—deified kings and heroes—objects of adoration and ceremonial worship. We did not find on either of the monuments or sculptured fragments any delineation of human, or, in fact, any other kind of sacrifice, but had no doubt that the large sculptured stone invariably found before each "idol" was employed as a sacrificial altar. The form of sculpture most frequently met with was a death's head, sometimes only accessory; whole rows of them on the outer wall, adding gloom to the mystery of the place, keeping before the eyes of the living death and the grave, presenting the idea of a holy city—the Mecca or Jerusalem of an unknown people.

John L. Stephens
Incidents of Travel in Central America, Chiapas and Yucatan

Copán, in western Honduras, is the southernmost major center of the lowland Maya. The site lies within one of the richest and most consistently fertile river valleys of the whole Maya area, at an altitude just over two thousand feet. The landscape is lush and rolling; pine forests rise on the nearby mountainsides. The site has been settled since early Preclassic times. The Copán River has cut away a large section of the Acropolis, exposing many successive layers of earlier construction.

In layout, Copán most closely resembles a Petén ceremonial center. It is a world of open space and volume, with temples set above courts and great plazas. Nevertheless, the real force of the site emanates from its carved monuments, not its architecture. The stelae and altars are set prominently in open spaces, which they seem to dominate in both spirit and stature. These monuments were carved from soft green trachyte that has hardened upon exposure to air and turned a delicate gray. The stelae are usually about twelve feet high; the altars set before them stand from two to three feet high, and measure three to four feet across.

The cumulative effect of these monuments creates the unique mood of Copán—a static, unchanging world of animistic forces dominated by the figures carved on the stelae. In these, the visible fact of power and superiority seems more important than any specific individual characterization. The figures were probably intended to portray important members of Copán's elite. Although no dynastic sequence has yet been established for Copán, glyphs from the back of Stela A do show that the most important ruler of nearby Quiriguá was a member of an elite family of Copán. It would be very surprising if no other personal or dynastic histories were recorded on Copán's monuments.

The first Long Count inscriptions at Copán date from the late fifth century A.D., but construction of the first level of the Ball Court indicates that ceremonial life was well developed at the site by at least the end of the third century A.D. During its later development, particularly during the seventh and eighth centuries, Copán stood foremost among Maya centers in advances in astronomical knowledge and important innovations in calendrical computations. During the eighth century, when Copán sculptors achieved their most accomplished monumental works, the major temples were decorated with unusually beautiful carving, often in the full round, which formed an integral part of the architectural design. Little of this carving is, however, visible today; as a result of the weak mortar used in the construction of the buildings and of the earthquakes which have plagued the site, only the lower portions of a few temples now remain standing.

The monumental sculpture is therefore all the more striking today. The stelae have been reinforced and reset in their original position, and exert an almost magnetic attraction upon the visitor. Each mysterious carved figure draws the onlooker and demands his full attention. But for the most part the monuments do not convey the intimacy that the viewer might expect. Instead their impressive ornateness and static impassivity create distance. Like a great temple of Tikal, Copán's stelae attest to the superiority and divine command of the elite, and the onlooker feels humble, even uneasy, before them.

The carving of the altars intensifies this mood, for to the contemporary mind they are inscrutable and grotesque, nightmare creatures of a surreal imagination. However, their very strangeness provides an important key to understanding the monuments as a whole. The monuments clearly do not portray reality in any naturalistic sense. It was not the task of the sculptor to copy reality but, rather, to carve symbols which would actualize in some form the incomprehensible, supraearthly forces of the universe. In this sense, even the figures portrayed on these stelae—the "true men," the rulers—can be seen as agents of magical, divine force. As mediators with the gods, they were responsible both for the continued well-being of the physical universe and for Maya society.

Although there were set ritualistic patterns for the glorified portrayal of Copán's elite members, the sculptors did find room for considerable innovation and fantasy in the carving of the elaborate ornamentation and dress of the stelae figures. The unique deep-relief carving of Copán undoubtedly resulted in part from readily available soft volcanic stone, but the ritualistic frontal stance of the figures must have been set by a deliberate, early choice of either an imaginative ruler or a bold sculptor. Although the three-dimensional sculptural style of the stelae approaches carving in the full round, even on the latest stelae the back of the human figure disappears into the stone shaft bearing the hieroglyphic inscriptions. Only in the decoration of Copán's eighth-century architectural projects were the sculptors given the freedom to carve in absolutely full round. These works were decorated with many different human-divine figures, using the silhouette of the figure itself to define sculptural form against open space.

The development and achievements of the unusual stela tradition that reached its peak at Copán during the eighth century A.D. have been assessed and evaluated over the years in strikingly different ways. To Herbert Spinden, the first scholar to chart a developmental, stylistic analysis of Maya monuments, Stela H, for example, seemed the perfect stela at Copán, the culmination of a great tradition. To the art historian Paul Westheim, on the other hand, Stela H was hardly more than a figurine or dress model. Westheim maintained that even though there was perfection in the carving technique of Copán, there was also a certain decadence in its artistic form. His rather harsh esthetic judgement was based upon the belief that the moment low-relief sculpture leaves a flat two-dimensional plane and establishes actual three-dimensional depth without fully achieving sculptural form in the full round, the relief loses its inherent internal tension and its specific expressivity as a genre.

Westheim further suggested that the elaborate and often confusing deep-relief sculpture of Copán was an increasingly precious and decadent feudal art which clearly signaled the final collapse of Classic Maya civilization. The development of a late, baroque-like style in Maya sculpture is interesting in itself, but its being found at only one ceremonial center seems hardly to justify its application to Maya culture as a whole. The last inscriptions of Copán date around A.D. 800, and it is most peculiar that the fertile Copán valley should be the scene of one of the first significant collapses of the Classic Maya centers. But it is also true that western sites such as Palenque and Yaxchilán, both known for their outstanding examples of disciplined low-relief carving, dedicated their last monuments around the close of the eighth century. Perhaps more important than the difference in styles may be the fact that Copán, like Palenque on the west, is situated on a frontier of the Maya lowland culture, and it may have been undermined at the close of the Classic Period by non-Maya influences.

Whatever the reasons for its cultural decline, the Copán valley was not depopulated at the end of the Classic Period. Postclassic pottery has been found in burial tombs within the abandoned temple buildings, indicating some continued ceremonial activity, but there is no evidence of any attempt to continue erecting monuments, as at Tikal. Instead, plain and carved stones alike were used in the construction of the burial tombs, and the Postclassic survivors made sporadic offerings at the base of stelae remaining in their original positions.

What the heritage of Copán leaves us is difficult to summarize and assess. By virtue of its nonconformist sculptural style and many undeciphered hieroglyphic inscriptions, it perhaps best exemplifies the wide range and unknown wealth of informative material hidden beneath the very forces the artists sought to clarify. Physically, artistically, and even emotionally, Copán remains a polar type, a unique challenge to the contemporary mind. Its mood and lavishness attract us; the intimacy of the site deepens our awareness and appreciation of the ancient Maya; but ultimately its commanding sculptural and religious traditions overwhelm us, firmly reestablishing the distance and superiority of the elite.

11. Stela 13 and its circular altar stand on an open hillside several miles east of Copán's Acropolis. Dedicated in A.D. 652, the stela and altar are typical of early monuments at the site. The carving is of comparatively low relief; the blocklike stela is decorated only with glyphs.

12. The Ball Court is prominently located between the Great Plaza on the north and the Court of the Heiroglyphic Stairway on the south. The court was built around A.D. 250, but its reconstructed form reflects its appearance in the eighth century.

13. *Two open vaults face one another across the Ball Court. The buildings on either side of the court were undoubtedly associated with the rituals of the ball game, which for the Maya and other pre-Hispanic cultures of Mesoamerica was an important religious ritual as well as an entertaining athletic event.*

14. The Reviewing Stand was dedicated in the late eighth century
A.D., and is named for the steps and platform, thought to resemble
a grandstand, which may have been used by members of the
aristocracy for viewing special ceremonies in the secluded West
Court.

15. Altar Q is one of two monuments standing in the West Court.
It was dedicated in A.D. 776. Its glyphic inscription and carved
figures are thought either to commemorate an important meeting
of Maya astronomers or to record a crucial development in the
dynastic history of Copán.

16. The flat stone slab known as Altar T is almost inconspicuous at the west end of the Hieroglyphic Court. The two-headed, croco-dile-like monster carved on its side combines mythological symbols of earth and water.

17. *The magnificent altar dedicated with Stela D in A.D. 736 represents a striking portrayal of the death god. It is carved with a grotesque face on each of two sides, this being the north side, facing the stela.*

18. The majority of Copán's eighth-century stelae and altars are grouped together in the Great Plaza. Stela D stands at the northern edge of the court; Stela C is on the right; Stela B, with only its south glyph panel visible, is on the left. The spherical altar in the foreground has the shape and characteristics of a sacrificial stone.

19. Slender Stela P, dedicated in A.D. 623, is the only stela in the West Court, and is probably the earliest one on the Copán Acropolis. The stiff body position and bulging oval eyes are characteristic of early sculptural treatment of the human figure at this site.

20. Stela 5, outside the protected archaeological site of Copán near the road to the village of Copán, was dedicated about A.D. 667. It has a figure carved on each of two sides; this view is of the west side.

21. *The carving of Stela B, dedicated in A.D. 731, is characteristic of the elaborate, deep-relief sculptural style that developed at Copán early in the eighth century. The ruler's face is naturalistically carved, but detailed, heavy ornament tends to obscure the body.*

22. *The back, or west side, of Stela B is decorated with a large stylized face. Stela C, with an altar in the shape of a two-headed turtle, stands at the center of the Great Plaza. Stela F and the peculiar, small G altars are on the Plaza's eastern side.*

23. The delicate carving of the figure on Stela A approaches the full round. The expressive face is sensitively protrayed, but the ruler's body proportions are strangely dwarfed. The stela, dedicated in A.D. 730, faces east toward Stela H.

24. *The robed figure of Stela H is thought to represent a female member of Copán's elite. Her position facing Stela A may indicate that she was related by marriage to the figure on that stela. The two stelae may have been dedicated together as a pair.*

25. *Stela N was dedicated in A.D. 761. Its extremely deep ornate relief indicates that it is perhaps the latest stela at Copán. The elaborately dressed ruler on its northern side overlooks the Court of the Hieroglyphic Stairway. The figure on its opposite side faces the stairway leading to Temple 11.*

26. The glyphs inscribed on the back of Stela F are carved in groups of four, each group enclosed within a rope loop and surrounded by deep grooves representing feathers. This unusual way of framing glyph blocks is known nowhere else.

27. All sides of the inscrutable altar accompanying Stela N are carved with the grotesque limbs and features of an unidentifiable mythological creature.

III. Quiriguá

The general character of these ruins is the same as at Copan. The monuments are much larger, but they are sculptured in lower relief, less rich in design, and more faded and worn.

John L. Stephens
Incidents of Travel in Central America, Chiapas and Yucatan

The sculptural style and hieroglyphic inscriptions of Quiriguá identify this small site as a satellite of Copán. It lies in eastern Guatemala, twenty-five miles north of Copán, in the fertile Motagua River valley into which the Copán River drains. Though increasingly visited today, the site is still characterized by a sense of neglect and an eerie, disquieting silence. Large, ungainly monuments dominate the small clearing surrounded by dense tropical growth, and the visitor has the peculiar sensation of being at the mercy of unknown forces, of being watched by unseen eyes.

Like Copán, Quiriguá is best known for its sculpture. Its rudely constructed buildings have all collapsed and are barely discernible beneath a heavy mantle of vegetation. The local red sandstone allowed the Quiriguá sculptors to adopt the distinctive style of deep-relief carving found at Copán. But for some reason the monuments at Quiriguá never achieved the richness and sophisticated three-dimensional quality of those at Copán. Although superb craftsmanship is evident in the carving of glyph details and complex animal and vegetal forms, the greatest emphasis at Quiriguá seems to have been placed upon the creation of large and imposing monuments which are more impressive for their size than for their sculptural qualities.

Comparative studies of hieroglyphs of these two neighboring sites have shown that Quiriguá became a ceremonial center of significance through the influence of a ruling family at Copán. Around A.D. 737 a young member of Copán's *caan,* or "sky" family, established a dynasty at Quiriguá which lasted about seventy-five years. During the fifty-year reign of Ruler I, most of the site's monumental sculpture was dedicated. Portrayals of Ruler I range from that of a pudgy-cheeked youth to the bearded, elongated face on the northern side of Stela E. Althogh he is recognizable on many stelae, there is little sense of his individuality or special qualities as ruler. He died sometime around A.D. 785, and was followed by a rapid succession of young monarchs. Soon after A.D. 800, Quiriguá, like Copán, ceased to dedicate sculpture, and ceremonial life in the Motagua River valley quickly reverted to simple agricultural rites.

28. *An early portrayal of the figure known as Ruler I appears on the west side of Stela J, dedicated in A.D. 756. He was the young member of Copán's "sky" family who inaugurated a family dynasty of Quiriguá and ruled the site for some fifty years.*

29. Stela E stands thirty-five feet high and is the tallest known stela erected by the Maya. It was dedicated in A.D. 771 and has a figure carved on each of two sides. The bearded face on the north side portrays Ruler I in his late forties.

IV. Yaxchilán

"There it is!" said the old Indian to his son and grandson. "There is Yaxchilán." They were standing on the top of a hill, and the trail wound down to the plain spread at their feet. There in the distance the sacred city of Yaxchilán rose above the river valley. The temples of the gods and the houses and palaces of the priests and rulers rose up from a skirt-like slope of a hill. From the great Usumacinta River to the very top of the hill could be seen magnificent buildings, adorned with designs painted in beautiful, vivid colors.

After resting for a moment, they went down the hill and on their way to the sacred city. On all the other paths more Indians were approaching. All of them carried on their backs their supplies as well as their offerings for the gods. Also coming, commanded by merchants, were long lines of Indians carrying salt from the far coast of Yucatan. Others came with loads of cacao beans, the currency of the Maya, from Soconusco, on the Pacific coast, while still others came with tanned skins of jungle animals, or with clay vessels adorned with colored figures depicting historic scenes, or birds, or monkeys. The servants of the nobles were shouting for the way to be opened for the litters of their masters. There was great confusion and a tumult of nervous activity on all the paths which led to Yaxchilán.

They crossed the Usumacinta in dugouts and eagerly landed at the foot of the hill of the sacred city. Clouds of incense rose towards the skies and the rhythm of the "tunkules," or drums made of hollow wood, mixed with the prayerful songs of the worshippers. The multitude of people from all parts of the Maya lowlands thronged before the temples. And the gods—of the sun, of rain, of corn, of war, and of death—were seated immutable and serene, their images carved in stone.

This was around one thousand five hundred years ago. Now this mysterious city is hidden in the heart of the jungle of the Tzendales in the state of Chiapas.

Frans Blom
"Yaxchilán, la ciudad maravillosa de los mayas"

Yaxchilán, in extreme southeastern Mexico, is situated within a large bend of the upper Usumacinta River, which here forms the boundary between Mexico and Guatemala. Its temple structures are built on the slope of a hill standing 450 feet high overlooking the Usumacinta and the Petén rain forest of Guatemala. Yaxchilán is still one of the most inaccessible and untouched Maya lowland sites. Except for a few foot trails and some clearing around the major temples, it remains entirely shrouded beneath dense jungle growth. Enormous ceibas, the holy tree of the Maya, tower above the site, and thick vegetation threatens to destroy many of the temples that have miraculously survived centuries of abandonment.

Yaxchilán's temples show a thick-walled block masonry construction similar to that used in the Petén. The structural solidity of the surviving buildings is due largely to the use of stone lintels above the doorways. The wooden lintels used at other Maya sites inevitably decayed, either weakening or completely destroying the building facade, but many of Yaxchilán's stone lintels are still in place and the temples intact. One of the most impressive and best-preserved structures is Temple 33. All three of its beautifully carved stone lintels are in place over the low doorways, and even the latticed frame of its long roof comb still stands.

Temple 33, like many of Yaxchilán's structures, consists of only one vaulted chamber. One unusual innovation is the use of inner partitions, which act as interior buttresses distributing the weight of the large roof comb. On the whole, however, the architecture of Yaxchilán is of a simple nature. There are no massive temple-pyramids but, instead, many small temples standing on different levels of the terraced hillside.

Yaxchilán's outstanding achievement is without question its immense production of beautifully carved low-relief sculpture. As a result of extensive exploration at the site around 1900, Teobert Maler reported a total of twenty stelae and forty-six lintels at Yaxchilán. Almost all these monuments were executed in a strong low-relief style that is matched in its excellence only by the carving at Piedras Negras and Palenque. Several of the more beautiful lintels were transported by Alfred Maudslay to the British Museum at the end of the nineteenth century; numerous Yaxchilán monuments are to be found in the National Museum of Anthropology in Mexico City. But at the site, there is still a considerable amount of magnificent sculpture, much of it in need of precautionary measures to protect it from further erosion.

Tatiana Proskouriakoff has recently shown that a significant number of Yaxchilán's monuments provide an almost narrative historical account of the Jaguar clan's rule at the site. She found that, unlike the stelae of Piedras Negras, which were dedicated at regular five-year intervals and inscribed with glyphic records of reigns and pertinent dates in the lives of the rulers and their families, the lintels of Yaxchilán were dedicated at irregular intervals and were carved with scenes actually depicting historical events.

The earliest known inscription at Yaxchilán is dated A.D. 454, but it was not until around A.D. 680 that Shield Jaguar, the first of the Jaguar dynasty, became ruler. During a long reign that lasted until he was well into his nineties, he established a strong family line that became well known for militaristic conquest. Upon his death in A.D. 741, there was apparently considerable contention about the right of succession, with various persons claiming legitimacy through his descendants. Finally, in A.D. 752, a man known as Bird Jaguar was inaugurated as ruler, possibly having established his right to rule through warfare.

Whatever the circumstances of his accession, Bird Jaguar's sixteen-year reign was less militaristic than that of Shield Jaguar, and under his direction Yaxchilán reached the height of its artistic production. Bird Jaguar apparently concentrated more on the social aspects of administration and diplomacy than on overt conquest, strengthening his power by distributing honors and by granting positions of status for important families.

Lintel 42, dedicated at the time of Bird Jaguar's accession in A.D. 752, shows him negotiating a family alliance. Other lintels show him commemorating such events as marriage arrangements, property settlements, and military victories. Proskouriakoff believes that particularly significant is the scene depicted on Lintel 2 of Temple 33. Dedicated in A.D. 757, this lintel shows Bird Jaguar with the five-year-old descendant of Shield Jaguar. Both figures are depicted holding the symbolic staff of the ruler on the anniversary of Bird Jaguar's accession. Considering the evidence of this lintel and the dominating site of Temple 33, Proskouriakoff suggests that this temple may commemorate recognition of Shield Jaguar's descendant as successor to Bird Jaguar.

Bird Jaguar continued to rule until about A.D. 768, and died sometime before A.D. 771. Shield Jaguar's descendant would have been barely twenty years old when he took power in A.D. 771. Like his ancestor, the young ruler was apparently most interested in militaristic conquest. It was probably during his reign that nearby Bonampak was most strongly influenced by Yaxchilán. The militaristic scenes of Bonampak's murals may well reflect the dominating traditions of the larger site. Shield Jaguar's descendant paid little attention to the arts and to building projects at Yaxchilán, and during his reign hieroglyphic texts became less clear and the quality of the sculpture declined. Lintel 10 provides the last known inscription of Yaxchilán, a date equivalent to A.D. 807, by which time Shield Jaguar's descendant was probably no longer in power.

The reasons for the collapse of Classic Period civilization at Yaxchilán are not well understood, but are probably related both to internal tensions generated by the site's militaristic traditions and to intrusive foreign influences moving up the Usumacinta River. Offerings, especially the burning of the sacred copal resin, certainly continued to be made in the temples after the abandonment of the site. Even in recent times the Lacandón Maya have continued to make pilgrimages to Yaxchilán in order to venerate their principal god, Hachakyum, in Temple 33.

But for the most part, the site has suffered from unfortunate neglect and abuse, even at the hands of Mexico's archaeological authorities. One specific example is that of Stela 11, the last one still standing in its original position. In 1965 it was removed in an unsuccessful attempt to transport it by plane to the National Museum of Anthropology in Mexico City. After this project failed, rather than being protected in some way or returned to its original site, the stela was left exposed to flooding of the Usumacinta River. Thanks to the efforts of Gertrude Duby Blom, widow of archaeologist Frans Blom, it was eventually transported back to Yaxchilán, where it now is protected although not properly maintained. What remains at Yaxchilán has survived either by chance or through the personal efforts of a few concerned individuals. With increased concern on the part of the Mexican government and the appropriation of substantial funds for its preservation, Yaxchilán may finally receive suitable maintenance and attention. It is a site certainly worthy of careful preservation if not extensive excavation.

30. The three beautiful doorway lintels of Temple 33 bear inscriptions dating within five years of one another, and indicate the temple was dedicated around A.D. 755. Although most of the structure's facade decoration has fallen away, a large stucco figure still remains in place at the center of the long roof comb.

31. The roof comb of Temple 20 stands almost even with the temple's front wall, creating the illusion of a high front facade on the small one-roomed structure. A large stucco figure was once set in the roof comb niche above the doorway.

32. Lintel 42 is still in place in Temple 42, high above the
Usumacinta River. Dedicated in A.D. 752, the lintel shows the ruler
Bird Jaguar at the time of his accession with an ally who is easily
identified on other monuments by the unusual feature of a
mustache.

33. *Lintel 2, of Temple 33, shows Bird Jaguar in A.D. 757 with the five-year-old descendant of Shield Jaguar. Both royal figures are portrayed with the ruler's staff, possibly indicating that Shield Jaguar's descendant was to reign after Bird Jaguar.*

34. Lintel 3, also still in place in Temple 33, bears an inscription dated A.D. 756. Bird Jaguar stands on the right, facing an important ally, who, like the ruler, holds a manikin scepter, the symbol of authority.

35. This sculptural fragment is part of Stela 7, dedicated in A.D. 771. The stela marks the completion of Katun 17, the twenty-year period from A.D. 751 to 770, and commemorates the accession of Shield Jaguar's descendant as ruler of Yaxchilán.

36. *Lintel 22 is remarkable for its rows of delicately carved small glyphs. It is one of the oldest pieces of sculpture at Yaxchilán, probably dating from the fifth century A.D.*

37. *Lintel 27 is well concealed by jungle growth. The small glyphs
on its east side are barely discernible.*

38. *Many badly eroded sculptural fragments, such as these identified as possible pieces of Stela 4, lie scattered throughout the
unexcavated area of Yaxchilán.*

V. Bonampak

Bonampak is a small, compact site in Mexico about twenty miles southwest of Yaxchilán. It lies like a small jewel in the forest, within an hour's walk from the Lacanhá River. Not until 1946 was the building containing three rooms of unique murals first shown to a white man by the Lacandón Maya. Unfortunately, the murals are now scarcely visible, but the carving of the low-relief sculpture at Bonampak ranks with the finest of the Maya lowlands.

Some of Bonampak's early sculpture reveals the influence of Piedras Negras, but later works closely resemble those found at Yaxchilán. The most distinguishing trait of the Bonampak style is the deep depression or rounded cut representing the iris of the human eye in many figures, notably the large one of Stela 1.

Although Stela 1 has broken into several pieces, its two largest intact fragments still give an idea of how impressive the entire original stela was. J. Eric Thompson believes it was dedicated around A.D. 780, whereas Tatiana Proskouriakoff gives it a stylistic dating around A.D. 810, after the painting of the murals. It is a proud, flamboyant work, decidedly different in feeling from Stela 2, which is close in its concept and technique to the sculpture of Yaxchilán.

Dedicated in A.D. 785, Stela 2 shows two women flanking a ruler. Like the women portrayed in the murals, these clearly have important social and ceremonial roles. The prominence of women in the rituals of Bonampak is no doubt another reflection of influence from Yaxchilán, where the sculpture indicates that they had a more significant role in ceremonial life than at other Maya ceremonial centers.

39. Stela 1 dates from the late eighth century and is one of the largest stelae dedicated by the Maya, originally measuring about sixteen feet high and eight feet wide. The stela base stands upright in its original position. The large piece in the foreground shows the proud elite figure portrayed on the upper part of the monument.

40. Stela 2 is one of two stelae set on the stairway leading to the
small temples of Bonampak. Dedicated in A.D. 785, it depicts a
ruler who is flanked on either side by beautifully robed women.

VI. Palenque

Ancient Palenque not only looks up from below at a screen of surrounding hills . . . it also looks down like an eagle from its aerie over the wide expanse of a world below. The range of forest-clad mountains into which it is set does not decrease gently in rolling foothills to the plains; its base falls abruptly, like a coastal escarpment standing out against the level sea. Surmounting it is a narrow flat shelf that rims the irregular summits of the range. This shelf penetrates back between the hills in a series of narrow pockets, and in one such pocket are the main ruins of Palenque. Little streams from the mountains above cross the terrace at short intervals to fall from its brink in a confusion of tumbling cascades below. Several of the rivers of Tabasco, which is a country of rivers, have sources here.

To add emphasis to this dramatic opposition of mountain and plain, the lowlands seem to reach their lowest just at the foot of the escarpment. A narrow wooded valley, extending indefinitely in either direction, forms a moat outside it. Your first view of the ancient city is across this valley from a ridge on the opposite side. Through a gap in the trees, you see a small square clearing on the dark scarp of the mountains confronting you, and in it a compact group of stone buildings that glints like a jewel in the sunlight. Unlike all the other ruined sites of Middle America, most of which stand at hazard in the midst of broad plains or valleys, this one seems to hang on the mountainside, as if not men but eagles had selected it for their abode.

Louis J. Halle, Jr.
River of Ruins

Palenque, one of the westernmost Maya lowland centers, is situated in the transitional area between the southern rain forest and the northern savanna. It lies within the area of the heaviest rainfall of the Maya lowlands, and is bordered on all sides by thick jungle. In developing the site, the Maya made use of two striking innovations that enabled them to live more comfortably with the area's excessive rainfall. Most important was an unusually open and airy architectural style. Also crucial was a carefully planned water system, in which an underground aqueduct prevented flooding of the site during the rainy season by carrying off excess water.

The natural advantages of Palenque's geographical situation are readily apparent.

Pure water was always available from the spring at the foot of the sierra, and the surrounding forest supplied wood, fruits, wild game, and the important sacrificial copal resin. Below the site stretches the fertile lowland plain, and behind it stand sheer cliffs, providing natural protection as well as a variety of stone for building and sculpture. The Maya's adaptation to this rich environment resulted in cultural achievements of the highest order. At no other ceremonial center except Copán is the presence of the ancient elite so strongly felt today.

Although Palenque was occupied intermittently during the first several centuries before Christ, it was not until around the fourth century A.D. that a fixed population established itself there permanently. During its Early Classic Period, A.D. 317–593, there were strong ties with Piedras Negras and probably other major centers to the east. Palenque lies within the drainage area of the lower Usumacinta, about thirty miles west of the river, so that its natural avenue of communication and trade was along this important water route. As one of the westernmost Maya centers within easy reach of the Gulf of Mexico, Palenque also had continuous contact with the settlements along the coast. Fragments of ball-game yokes and carvings of flattened stone heads typical of the Totonac or Tajín culture, near present-day Veracruz, show that cultural influence from this area was particularly strong at the close of the Classic Period.

The period of highest cultural achievement at Palenque spanned a shorter length of time than at other southern Maya centers. There is no evidence of either hieroglyphic inscriptions or major corbel vaulted temples from the Early Classic Period. But sometime around A.D. 593 a highly developed culture emerged, and the greatest achievements of Palenque were accomplished between the earliest and latest known inscriptions on the sculpture, dates equivalent to A.D. 610 and A.D. 783. No major stela tradition developed at Palenque, perhaps because of an independent religious cult or perhaps merely because the dolomite used for the sculpture was most suitable for low-relief carving and delicate incision of the surface. Both the large panels in the temples and the tablets in the Palace complex were conceived as integral parts of the architecture, the former depicting religious motifs and the latter commemorating the more secular activities of the court.

The seventh century saw intense religious activity at Palenque and the dedication of three beautiful small temples—the Temple of the Sun, the Temple of the Cross, and the Temple of the Foliated Cross—as well as the construction of the great funerary monument, the Temple of the Inscriptions. All these temples stand prominently atop pyramids built upon natural rises of the terrain, but the pyramid bases of Palenque, in contrast to those of Tikal, are not so high as to dwarf the temples built upon them.

The architecture itself incorporated several distinctive innovations, one of the most important of which was the use of the upper building facade as a sloped, overhanging mansard roof to direct torrential rainfall away from the building. The temple facades were opened by the use of wide doorways, creating a kind of portico that assured adequate ventilation within the building. In most structures, the use of parallel vaults separated by a thin inner wall allowed the construction of unusually wide rooms; in the Palace complex, double vaults were extended to create spacious halls or galleries.

Palenque is best known for the magnificent Royal Tomb that Alberto Ruz discovered below the Temple of the Inscriptions. The tradition of burying important persons within temple-pyramids is known from other ceremonial centers, but nowhere in the Maya lowlands has a more magnificent tomb or funerary monument been discovered. The burial vault lies some five feet below ground level and is reached only by a seventy-five-foot vaulted stairway within the solid core of the pyramid. The burial chamber was apparently constructed first, and the pyramid and temple were built over it to form a grand funerary monument. It may have been constructed during the lifetime of the ruler-priest buried within it; once the body was interred, the vaulted stairway was filled with rubble and the tomb sealed.

Six young sacrificial victims were buried at the entrance to the tomb. About one thousand pieces of jade were found within the sarcophagus. The skull of the ruler-priest was covered with a mask of jade mosaic, and his remains were richly adorned with exquisite jade ornaments. By all indications, the divine ruler continued to be venerated after his death. Death for the Maya represented only a change in one's state of being, and evidently this ruler's spirit played an important role in the continuing ceremonial life of Palenque:

> A serpent modeled in lime plaster seems to rise straight out of the sarcophagus and ascend the steps which lead to the threshold of the room. Here it is transformed into a tube, running as far as the flooring of the corridor and after this it leads on to the temple, in the form of an echeloned moulding, hollow and superimposed on the steps. This amounts to a magical union, a conduit for the spirit of the dead man to ascend to the temple in order that the priests might continue to be in contact with his deified being and be able to explain his mandates.

> Alberto Ruz Lhuiller, in *Conquistadores without Swords*

Palenque's priests probably continued for some time the religious traditions associated with the great ruler, but without his active physical leadership the emphasis of ceremonial life seems to have gradually shifted from purely religious ritual to the more secular activities of the court. It is perhaps significant that Palenque's outstanding accomplishments during the eighth century were works of sculpture depicting the aristocratic ceremonies of the elite.

The courtly mood of the Palace complex prevails most strongly at Palenque today. Its airy spaces and sculptured monuments reflect the presence of the elite within its walls. But probably it was the divine priest-king who influenced the brief, aristocratic life of Palenque most deeply, and the enduring appeal and mystery of the site are intensified in untold ways by our awareness of the tomb of this great man.

Perhaps a dissident hierarchy or the disintegration of cultural and religious traditions finally weakened the power of Palenque's elite and set the stage for a foreign intrusion. Within about one hundred years after the death of the great ruler-priest, the dominance of Palenque was finally undermined by foreign cultures from along the Gulf coast. The last known inscription of the site, dated A.D. 799, appears on a painted ceramic vessel. Carved stone heads and other artifacts of Gulf coast cultures found at the site indicate a brief period of Postclassic occupation by outsiders, but Palenque was soon abandoned to the dense vegetation of the jungle.

Like Machu Picchu, the untouched Inca citadel isolated deep in the highlands of southern Peru, Palenque is a world unto itself. The feeling it engenders was probably best expressed by Stephens in 1841:

> In the romance of the world's history nothing ever impressed me more forcibly than the spectacle of this great and lovely city, overturned, desolate, and lost; discovered by accident, overgrown with trees for miles around, and without even a name to distinguish it. Apart from everything else, it was a mourning witness to the world's mutations.
>
> *Incidents of Travel in Central America, Chiapas and Yucatán*

41. *The view from the Temple of the Inscriptions overlooks Palenque's Palace Complex and north group of buildings. The reconstructed square tower dominating the Palace's labyrinthine arrangement of interior courts, galleries, and chambers may have been used as both watchtower and observatory.*

42. The north court, the largest and probably the latest of the
Palace courts, was apparently finished during the eighth century,
when courtly life reached its height at Palenque. Enigmatic large
figures on either side of the stairway of Palace House A define the
eastern edge of the court.

43. *The largest temple at Palenque is the Temple of the Inscriptions, known since 1952 to be an elaborate funerary monument honoring the great ruler-priest buried beneath the sixty-five-foot-high pyramid. Both the temple and the tomb are thought to have been dedicated in the late seventh or early eighth century A.D.*

44. *The Temple of the Sun is the best preserved of the three small temples grouped together around a plaza on the eastern side of Palenque. Some traces of stucco decoration are still visible, and the entire frame of the delicate roof comb remains intact.*

45. *The Temple of the Sun faces directly east across the plaza to the Temple of the Foliated Cross. The architectural plan of the two temples is identical, but the front half of the Temple of the Foliated Cross has collapsed, leaving the openings to its rear vault visible.*

46. The wall bordering the west side of the Palace's north court is decorated with a few relief carvings. The striking glyph block on the right measures approximately a foot on each side.

47. *The oval plaque still in place in a wall of Palace House E portrays within a space about four feet by three feet a woman offering a crown with headdress to a seated ruler. The plaque dates from the late seventh or early eighth century A.D. The graceful ceremonial gesture reappears on two later eighth-century Palace tablets.*

48. The roughly carved figures on the eastern side of the Palace's north court are totally unlike the classically conceived figures of the Palace tablets. Kneeling, with one hand raised to the opposite shoulder as a sign of submission, these figures may represent a procession of slaves or subject peoples.

VII. Dzibilchaltún

If the number, grandeur, and beauty of its buildings were to count toward the attainment of renown and reputation in the same way as gold, silver, and riches have done for other parts of the Indies, Yucatán would have become as famous as Peru and New Spain have become, so many, in so many places, and so well built are they, it is a marvel; the buildings themselves, and their number, are the most outstanding thing that has been discovered in the Indies.

Because this country, a good land as it is, is not today as it seems to have been in the time of prosperity when so many great edifices were erected with no native supply of metals for the work, I shall put here the reasons I have heard given by those who have seen the works. These are that they must have been the subjects of princes who wished to keep them occupied and therefore set them to these tasks; or else that they were so devoted to their idols that these temples were built by community work; or else that since the settlements were changed and thus new temples and sanctuaries were needed, as well as houses for their lords, these being always constructed of wood and thatch; or again the reason lay in the ample supply in the land of stone, lime, and a certain white earth excellent for building use, so that it would seem an imaginary tale, save to those who have seen them.

Bishop Landa
Yucatán, Before and After the Conquest
William Gates, ed.

During Bishop Landa's time, the Yucatán Peninsula was known by the natives as "the land of deer and turkey." In spite of the semiarid climate, wild game abounded in the dense brush forest. Nevertheless, the living conditions of Yucatán can be extremely harsh, even today. Annual rainfall drops progressively from between seventy and ninety inches near the Petén to around eighteen inches at the northern tip of the peninsula. The rains usually occur between May and October, but severe drought sometimes ruins the staple corn crop upon which the farmers depend. Yucatán has no surface rivers and only a few lakes, for the rainfall penetrates quickly in the porous limestone shelf. Only where the surface has collapsed, providing access to underground rivers, are there large natural wells, or *cenotes,* which provide a dependable year-round water supply.

Early settlement naturally developed around these cenotes, as at Dzibilchaltún, a large site north of present-day Mérida. Dzibilchaltún was apparently settled around 1000 B.C., the earliest known settlement of the entire Maya lowlands. Few structures have survived the repeated fires and the continuous plundering of the area for construction material. Archaeological excavation has nevertheless shown that the site was continuously occupied from around 1000 B.C. until the time of the Spanish Conquest.

The director of excavations at Dzibilchaltún, the late E. Wyllys Andrews IV, found that the distinctive features associated with Classic Maya culture did not appear at Dzibilchaltún until around A.D. 500, and that from then until A.D. 900 the development of the site closely followed cultural traditions of the Petén. Evidence in the unbroken stratigraphy of the site indicated that Dzibilchaltún did not produce the great architectural monuments of its Florescent Period until after A.D. 900, a date which has traditionally been assumed to mark the close of the Maya Classic Period.

Other perplexing evidence Andrews encountered in the excavation of Dzibilchaltún was that of an extremely dense concentration of buildings within an area of some nineteen square miles. On the basis of house mounds, he estimated a population at the site between A.D. 500 and A.D. 900 in excess of one hundred thousand persons. This represents an unprecedented concentration of population for the ancient Maya, one which is approached only remotely by recent estimates of Late Classic Tikal. Although such an urban settlement could be explained partly by Dzibilchaltún's proximity to the coastal salt marshes, the merchandising of this important natural resource offers only a partial explanation for such densely concentrated settlement. The extensive ruins within the nineteen square miles of the archaeological site may actually represent a group of interconnected, heavily occupied centers rather than one major city. However, the explanation of an apparent population far in excess of what the surrounding agricultural land could support still remains undetermined.

49. *The Temple of the Seven Dolls is the most striking of Dzibilchaltún's few remaining structures. Constructed in the late fifth century A.D., with its peculiar square windows and unstable construction, it may have been an experimental form of northern architecture.*

VIII. Cobá

> The buildings of Cobá are in a sorry state of preservation, but there appear to have been temple-pyramids and palaces like those of the Petén. It continued to be inhabited into Post-Classic times, for there are a few structures like those of Tulum (a very late town on the east coast of the peninsula), and there are references to Cobá in late Maya legends in which the centre is associated with the Sun God.
>
> Michael Coe
> *The Maya*

Cobá, meaning in Maya something like "ruffled waters," is named for the shallow lakes around which the site developed. Although it lies deep within the forest of Quintana Roo, in northeastern Yucatán, Cobá's settlement pattern, along with its masonry construction and some twenty-three stelae dating from the seventh century A.D., clearly identify the site as a direct extension of Petén traditions. As such, it is a unique example of a Late Classic, Petén-style center in northern Yucatán, and is certainly indicative of the strong cultural influence exerted throughout the entire lowland area by the Petén Maya.

Cobá is an extensive site which actually consists of numerous outlying ceremonial groups joined to a central complex by the broad elevated causeways known in Maya as *sacbés*, or white roads. Sixteen or more of these sacbés have been found in the area, the longest running due west from the central complex of Cobá sixty-two miles to Yaxuná, a site twelve miles south of Chichén Itzá. The sacbés were used extensively in the Petén as well as in western Yucatán. Although these paved roads are all almost perfectly level, they must have been used entirely for travel by foot, for the Maya did not have wheeled vehicles or beasts of burden.

Most of Cobá's remains are well hidden by dense forest growth, but two of its great temple-pyramids tower imposingly above the trees. The pyramid known as Nohoch-Mul dominates an open clearing in Group B, and El Castillo, or Temple I, of the central complex rises directly above Lake Cobá and Lake Macanxoc. From the top of Temple I, one has an unobstructed view to the horizon in all directions, with the monotonous level of the brush forest broken occasionally in the distance only by the slight rises of mounds covering unexcavated buried temples.

The isolation of Cobá is such that the local Maya farmers still hold strongly to local traditions and ancient beliefs. At the foot of Temple I stands an eroded fragment of Stela 11, which is referred to by the villagers as El Rey, "the king." Though broken and badly eroded, this stone still holds a magical power for the present-day Maya as guardian of the forest. The caretaker of the ruins says that a candle is often lighted before the stone as an offering along with a prayer for success in hunting.

50. One of the more distinct remains at the vast, overgrown site of Cobá is the imposing temple-pyramid known as Nohoch-Mul. It was dedicated in the Late Classic Period, but remodeling of its temple structure in Tulum's Postclassic style reveals that Cobá was an important ceremonial center as late as the fourteenth century.

IX. The Puuc

The flat limestone plain of northern Yucatán is broken by a range of hills that starts near Campeche on the west coast of the peninsula, runs northeastward, and then turns to the southeast, forming an angle with its apex to the north. In the region defined by this angle, named the Puuc from the Maya word for hills, was developed a style of architecture conspicuous for its careful workmanship in stone. Facing stones are accurately squared, smoothly finished, and nicely fitted together. In section they are very thin, forming a veneer that adheres to the surface of the wall, the body of which is a monolithic mass of rubble and mortar. This technique is not limited to the Puuc region, but here, after a long development, it attained a consummate refinement.

Tatiana Proskouriakoff
An Album of Maya Architecture

The most important Puuc sites are Edzná, Sayil, Labná, Kabáh, and Uxmal, each of which displays a distinct form of the Puuc architectural style. Archaeological evidence indicates that Sayil, Labná, and Kabáh were probably inhabited only from around the eighth century until the early tenth century A.D. Edzná, however, apparently developed during Early Classic times, as earlier cultural traits derived from the Petén coexist with those typical of the Puuc style. Uxmal of course stands in a class by itself not only because of its incomparable architectural achievements but also because it seems to have been occupied both earlier and later than the neighboring sites of the northern Puuc area.

The comparatively late settlement of the northern Puuc was probably due to the lack of available surface water throughout most of the area. Although the hill region is extremely fertile, natural wells are scarce, and during the dry season the inhabitants depend for their water entirely upon rainfall accumulated in the *chultunes,* underground cisterns. It is therefore not surprising that the predominant sculptural motif decorating architectural facades of the Puuc buildings is the sky-serpent mask commonly identified as Chac, the rain god, for it was his benevolence which made the difference between survival and disaster for the inhabitants.

Perhaps because of the unquestioned importance of the rain god, the stela cult and the glorified portrayal of members of the elite never became major concerns of the Puuc ruler-priests. The few stelae found at Puuc sites are set on platforms apart from the main architectural groups, suggesting that stela dedication was probably limited to certain groups that chose to follow ancient traditions inherited from the south. While the carving of the few stelae is for the most part crude, the stonework of the veneer masonry and elaborate frieze decoration is usually of excellent craftmanship. The repeated motifs suggest that a mass-production system was used in carving the standardized decorative elements and that the individual blocks of stone were probably used interchangeably in forming the mosaic-like frieze patterns.

Some structures show an influence of southern Maya traditions, particularly in the use of stucco sculpture, but this kind of decoration was eventually replaced by the ornamental mosaic stonework that is the hallmark of the Puuc style. As a rule, the mosaic decoration is usually concentrated in the frieze area, and is separated from the plain lower wall of the facade by a continuous, projecting molding. One striking exception, however, is the Codz-Poop of Kabáh, in which the entire facade is decorated with stylized Chac masks. Although there are traces of paint on some Puuc structures, a finishing coat of plaster was not applied, for there were no irregularities in the stonework to be concealed.

The most imposing Puuc structures are known as chambered pyramids, the multistoried complexes built into the sides of earthen pyramids. At Edzná, for example, an unusual adaptation of the temple-pyramid includes rooms on the north, south, and west sides of each of the pyramid's five stories. At Sayil, the pyramidal core is considerably reduced in size and merely provides terraced support for three tiers of chambers. Sayil's Palace demonstrates that Puuc vaults can be unusually wide, measuring over fifteen feet across. The innovative use of cylindrical doorway columns further opens up these large chambers, and creates an overall effect of lightness in an otherwise heavy and overpowering structure.

In contrast to the organized acropolis plan of the southern Maya sites, the northern Puuc centers have vast open spaces between their major structures. There is a dispersed, haphazard arrangement of buildings, with little concern for their orientation either toward the cardinal directions or around a central plaza. Sacbés, or ceremonial causeways, were often used to connect important groups of buildings, as at Labná, or, as at Kabáh and Uxmal, to connect the separate ceremonial centers themselves.

Because of the lack of deciphered hieroglyphic inscriptions and of a well-established chronology for the northern Maya, little is known about when and under what conditions the distinctive Puuc architectural style developed. It apparently extended throughout most of the modern state of Yucatán, with basic elements of its design appearing as far east as Chichén Itzá by the seventh century A.D. The rudiments of the style may have appeared earlier on the northern plain than in the Puuc hills, but its greatest expression was unquestionably achieved in the inhospitable Puuc area, where mere survival might represent a considerable achievement.

It is not known exactly when or why the comparatively short-lived occupation of the Puuc region ended, but it is thought that the area was abandoned either just before or shortly after the Mexican intrusion into Yucatán during the late ninth or early tenth century. The appearance of Mexican-style sculpture at Kabáh and Uxmal indicates that influence from the north was prevalent in the Puuc hills before the foreigners firmly established themselves at Chichén Itzá. It may be that the Mexicans themselves brought about the abandonment of the Puuc region in order to consolidate their rule on the northern plain, or it may be that long-term successful occupation of the Puuc area proved unfeasible. Whatever the reasons for the decline, by the end of the tenth century the focus of Yucatán's ceremonial life had irreversibly shifted to Chichén Itzá, and the Puuc soon became virtually abandoned.

51. *Unlike other Puuc chambered pyramids, Edzná's dominant structure is built over a smaller temple-pyramid of the Petén type and overlooks a central plaza and compact acropolis. The five-story structure reaches a height of approximately one hundred feet at the top of its roof comb.*

52. Sayil's imposing Palace is given an expansive openness through the innovative use of cylindrical doorway columns. The frieze of the second story is decorated with the mosaic sculpture characteristic of the Puuc architectural style, though the small upside-down figure is a decorative motif known elsewhere only on Yucatán's east coast.

53. Set at the foot of the rolling Puuc hills, Labná's ceremonial archway and small temple-pyramid are separated from the Palace building by a vast plaza some two hundred yards across. During Late Classic times a paved causeway connected these distant architectural groups.

54. A stylized form of the Chac mask is relentlessly repeated on the 150-foot facade of Kabáh's palace-like structure, the Codz-Poop. Although the overall design does not have as striking an effect as do the individual motifs themselves, it is nevertheless a fitting symbolic expression of the Puuc Maya's utter dependence on the rain gods.

55. *Chac masks, detail of the Codz-Poop.*

X. Uxmal

The Maya of the present day, marveling at the monumental works of their forefathers, explain them only as works of magic or enchantment. Thus, they suppose that the temples and palaces of the great cities, such as Chichén Itzá and Uxmal, were raised by men who possessed supernatural powers. These men were lords of the elements, which obeyed them docilely. So, by means of a special whistle, the stones, large as they were, ranged themselves without any help, forming marvelous and beautiful buildings. Another whistle or magical formula drew the water, the wind, or the beneficence of the gods, which were then at the service of these men, in whom all sanctity and virtue were lodged. Once this virtue was lost, came the ruin of their power. It is even said that the monoliths with human effigies which we admire today are nothing but these same men of long ago, turned into stone by divine punishment. The Maya of today, in spite of centuries which separate them from these miraculous days, and the changes that have taken place in their basic conceptions, still preserve a vague feeling that some time they will again be as they were before, and then be able to repeat the feats of their ancestors.

Alfonso Villa Rojas
"The Yaxuná-Cobá Causeway"

Uxmal is the largest of the Puuc sites. Its unique architecture stands out not only as the finest expression of the Puuc style but also as one of the great achievements of Maya civilization. Its most imposing structures—the Governor's Palace, the Nunnery Quadrangle, and the Pyramid of the Magician—have all been carefully excavated and reconstructed. Still, the site retains a character and power all its own. In the Pyramid of the Magician, the reconstruction actually heightens the overwhelming power of the structure and intensifies the mystery surrounding its origin. More than ever, the structure strikes one as a practical and imaginative impossibility. It appears more the product of magical forces than of man's will, an impression perhaps best expressed by the Indian legend told Stephens concerning its origin:

There was an old woman who lived in a hut on the very spot now occupied by the structure on which this building is perched, opposite the Casa del Gobernador . . . who went mourning that she had no children. In her distress she one day took an egg, covered it with a cloth, and laid it away carefully in one corner of the hut. Every day she went to look at it, until one morning she found the egg hatched, and a criatura, creature, or baby, born. The old woman was delighted, and called it her son, provided it with a nurse, took good care of it, so that in one year it walked and talked like a man; and then it stopped growing. The old woman was more delighted than ever, and said he would be a great lord or king. One day she told him to go to the house of the gobernador and challenge him to a trial of strength. The dwarf tried to beg off, but the old woman insisted, and he went. The guard admitted him, and he flung his challenge at the gobernador. The latter smiled, and told him to lift a stone of three arrobas, or seventy-five pounds, at which the litte fellow cried and returned to his mother, who sent him back to say that if the gobernador lifted it first, he would afterward. The gobernador lifted it, and the dwarf immediately did the same. The gobernador then tried him with other feats of strength, and the dwarf regularly did whatever was done by the gobernador. At length, indignant at being matched by a dwarf, the gobernador told him that, unless he made a house in one night higher than any in the place, he would kill him. The poor dwarf again returned crying to his mother, who bade him not to be disheartened, and the next morning he awoke and found himself in this lofty building. The gobernador, seeing it from the door of his palace, was astonished, and sent for the dwarf, and told him to collect two bundles of cogoiol, a wood of a very hard species, with one of which he, the gobernador, would beat the dwarf over the head, and *afterward* the dwarf should beat him with the other. The dwarf again returned crying to his mother; but the latter told him not to be afraid, and put on the crown of his head a tortilla de trigo, a small thin cake of wheat flour. The trial was made in the presence of all the great men in the city. The gobernador broke the whole of his bundle over the dwarf's head without hurting the little fellow in the least. He then tried to avoid the trial on his own head, but he had given his word in the presence of his officers, and was obliged to submit. The second blow of the dwarf broke his scull in pieces, and all the spectators hailed the victor as their new gobernador. The old woman then died; but at the Indian village of Mani, seventeen leagues distant, there is a deep well, from which opens a cave that leads underground an immense distance to Mérida. In this cave, on the bank of a stream, under the shade of a large tree, sits an old woman with a serpent by her side, who sells water in small quantities, not for money, but only for a criatura or baby to give the serpent to eat; and this old woman is the mother of the dwarf. Such is the fanciful legend connected with this edifice; but it hardly seemed more strange than the structure to which it referred.

Incidents of Travel in Central America, Chiapas and Yucatán

Excavation has shown the Pyramid of the Magician actually to be the result of at least five separate stages of varied temple construction. The eclectic use of foreign motifs and styles in the construction of these temples reveals a cosmopolitan independence on the part of Uxmal's rulers. While the first temple of the Pyramid shows the appearance of Puuc architectural elements possibly as early as the end of the sixth century A.D., the four upper temples reveal the tendency of Uxmal's architects to incorporate non-Puuc features within their own distinct architectural tradition. The outstanding example of this tendency is the Chenes-style temple on the west side of the Pyramid. The appearance of Mexican motifs, particularly the representation of Tlaloc, the rain god, also indicates that Uxmal's elite was open to northern cultural traditions well before the Mexican intrusion into Yucatán in the ninth century. Some fifteen crude stelae do attest to the persistence of southern Maya traditions at Uxmal, but ceramic evidence of trade relations with the Petén area is virtually nonexistent, indicating that Uxmal was probably less actively connected to the southern sites than was Dzibilchaltún, which imported large amounts of Petén pottery.

Of great importance to the elite of Uxmal, however, must have been the building complexes known as quadrangles, enclosed forms of the traditional plaza or court. Of Uxmal's five known quadrangles, the Palomas, or dove group, is closest in form to the multileveled acropolis of the southern lowlands. The Nunnery Quadrangle shows the most accomplished and sensitive adaptation of the enclosed court. Although the courtyard of the Nunnery is bordered on each side by a long, rangelike building, the enclosed space does not produce a claustrophobic feeling. The court is open at the corners, and the north building is set back on a second story, as in the chambered-pyramid design, creating a sense of added depth and openness.

In spite of the imaginative name given it by the sixteenth-century Spanish, the actual use of the Nunnery Quadrangle remains unknown. In its final form, the ninety chambers of the complex could have been used in a number of different ways: as residential quarters of the elite, as a setting for ceremonial occasions or religious training, as administrative offices, or even as storerooms.

However they were used, the well-proportioned, elongated buildings of the Nunnery stand with the Governor's Palace as the finest expression of Uxmal's unique Puuc style. The visual emphasis of all these buildings is on an extended, low, horizontal line, one which clearly defines and balances architectural volume against open space.

On each structure, a broad continuous molding separates the fine mosaic stonework of the decorated frieze from the plain lower wall; a similar molding, usually in the form of a projecting cornice, appears at the upper edge of the frieze and the building.

The frieze area itself represents a careful integration of sculptural forms and architectural design. In the buildings of the Nunnery Quadrangle, for instance, the frieze, or upper facade, leans slightly outward, creating subtle visual effects both in the architectural line and in the mosaic sculpture. Architecturally, the slight outward tilt of the facade provides for perspective correction in the long horizontal lines of the convergent east and west buildings. Sculpturally, it deepens the shadows cast by the mosaic relief and, as in the east building, effectively dramatizes the grimacing Chac masks.

The long-nosed Chac rain-god mask appears as a prominent decorative motif on most of Uxmal's friezes. This large site was as dependent upon accumulated rainfall for its water supply as were the other northern Puuc sites. In the latest and most impressive structures of Uxmal, the rain-god mask was incorporated into an increasingly abstract frieze design. The long elaborate frieze of the Governor's Palace represents the culmination of this stylistic development. This frieze is decorated with a continuous abstract pattern dominated by regularly rising and falling stepped lines. Stylized Chac masks, stepped frets, and Greek frets stand out as the prominent motifs of these alternating lines. The juxtaposition of the religious sky-serpent symbol against abstract, geometric forms creates a striking visual tension within the well-ordered rhythm of the design.

Unlike the symmetrically balanced frieze of the Governor's Palace, the frieze decoration of the west Nunnery building shows a cluttered array of different cultural motifs, among which Mexican phallic symbols and the Feathered Serpent figure prominently. The intrusion of these motifs into the Puuc design provides striking visual evidence of increasingly dominant Mexican influence in Yucatán at the close of the Classic Period. Uxmal shows signs of more prolonged Mexican influence than do other northern Puuc centers. Nonetheless, except for the appearance of the Mexican motifs, the Maya character of the site remains unchanged. The northern foreigners did not have either the desire or the opportunity to establish themselves for any length of time at Uxmal. Instead, they concentrated their forces at Chichén Itzá, which, as the focus of Mexican-dominated cultures, became the most prominent Postclassic center of Yucatán.

56. *The back, or east side, of the Pyramid of the Magician rises with sheer volcanic massiveness to a height of about 126 feet. The unique elliptical pyramid has been completely resurfaced with facing stone, intensifying the structure's awesome defiance of human scale.*

57. The main temple of the Pyramid of the Magician is built in the Chenes style, with the temple doorway forming the gaping mouth of a large serpent mask. The long temple directly above it dates from the final era of building activity at Uxmal. The temple remains extending along the base of the pyramid were once part of an early Puuc structure which formed the eastern side of an enclosed quadrangle.

58. The main entrance to the large enclosed quadrangle known as the Palomas, or dove, group is located at the center of its northern building. Above the vaults of this northern building is the long serrated roof comb thought by Stephens to resemble a dovecote, from which the quadrangle takes its name.

59. The western side of the Pyramid of the Magician overlooks the asymmetrical Nunnery Quadrangle. Its four separate buildings enclose a courtyard that is narrower on its northern end than on the south, where the main entranceway is located.

60. *The west Nunnery building is considered the latest structure of the Nunnery Quadrangle. The Mexican motifs added to the frieze design testify to the presence of strong Mexican influence during the final period of Uxmal's ceremonial life.*

61. A painted capstone in a vault of the east Nunnery building
provides an uncertain dedicatory date of A.D. 909 for the building.
The simplicity of the frieze makes it one of the finest examples of
Puuc design.

62. *The Governor's Palace stands upon a 23-foot artificial platform and faces to the east over a broad open terrace. The building's 326-foot facade stands out sharply against open space and is broken into three distinct sections by two steeply vaulted archways.*

63. The twenty-five-foot archways of the Governor's Palace originally served as open passages to either side of the building, but
they were later blocked by a cross wall and transformed into small
chambers entered through a columned portico. Over the centuries, however, the outside portico walls have collapsed, leaving the
arches visible again.

64. *The House of the Turtles is finished with a veneer masonry that ranks with the finest examples of Puuc stonework.*

XI. Chichén Itzá

An Old Maya Song

. . . . A tender boy was I at Chichén, when the evil man, the master of the army, came to seize the land. Woe! At Chichén Itzá heresy (idolatry) was favored.[1] YULU UAYANO![2] Ho! 1 Imix was when the ruler was seized at Chikin-chen.[3] Ho! Where thou art, there is the god. Ho! 1 Imix was the day he said this. At Chichén Itzá heresy was favored! Yulu uayano! Buried, buried! This was their cry. Buried, buried! . . . Woe! Woe! Woe! YULU UAYANO! Is there perhaps anyone who by chance has awakened? Force was brought to bear for the second time.[4] Woe! For the third time was established the religious festival of our enemies, our enemies. UUIYAO![5] Soon it will come to Chichén Itzá, (where) heresy was favored. YULU UAYANO! (In) the third heaven is the sun.[6] Behold! Who am I among men? I am a leafy covering. Eya! Who am I among the people of the Putun?[7] You do not understand me. EYA! I was created in the night. What were we born? EYA! We were like tame animals (to) Mizcit Ahau.[8] (But) an end comes to his roguery. Behold, so I remember my song. Heresy was favored. YULU UAYANO! EYA I die, he said because of the town festival.[9] EYA! I shall come, he said because of the destruction of the town. This is the end (of what is) in his mind, of what he thought in his heart. Me, he did not destroy. I tell what I have remembered in my song. Heresy was favored. YULU UAYANO! This is all of the song, the completion of the message of the Lord God.[10]

The Book of the Chilam Balam of Chumayel
Translation and notes by Ralph Roys

1. Here we have a reference to an old legend related to the first Spanish settlers, probably by Gaspar Antonio. 'It is told that the first inhabitants of Chichén Itzá were not idolators until Kukulcan, a Mexican captain, entered these provinces. He taught them idolatry, as they say it was he who taught them.' (Relaciones de Yucatan I, 270)
2. Old Toltec interjection of sorrow.
3. Literally, west-well, . . . likely some locality near Chichén Itzá.
4. According to the Mani and Tizimin Chronicles the conquest of Chichén by the Itzá in Katun 4 Ahau (967–987) was their second occupation of the city.
5. UUIYAO: probably an interjection. It might mean hunger or famine.
6. Probably a chronological statement, referring to the position of the sun at the time. The sky was divided into thirteen layers or heavens. . . .
7. Putun is a geographical term and refers to the people living near Laguna de Terminos, in the ancient province of Tixchel. . . .
8. Possibly one of the conquerors associated with Hunac Ceel.
9. Possibly a reference to human sacrifice.
10. Except, perhaps, for some of the prophecies which may have been sung, we have here a unique example of the old songs of the Maya. It was probably little understood in the eighteenth century when the Chumayel was compiled.

Significantly, Chichén Itzá consists of two distinct sections. At the northern end of the site, closest to the Sacred Cenote, stand the imposing structures dating from the period of Mexican occupation. To the south, separated from the northern complex by the highway running from Mérida to the east coast of Yucatán, lie the buildings of the Maya Classic Period. The name Chichén Itzá, meaning literally "the mouth of the well of the Itzá," refers to the Postclassic occupation of the site by the Itzá tribe. But who the Itzá were and when they actually occupied Chichén are still matters of considerable debate. They may have been a Mexicanized, non-Classic Maya group from along the Gulf coast. They are thought either to have been a part of the strong Mexican influence at Chichén Itzá between A.D. 900 and 1200 or to have ruled the site after the Mexican Period, from the early thirteenth century until the mid-fifteenth century.

Although little is known about the development of Chichén Itzá during the Early Classic Period, it is apparent that by around A.D. 600 it had become a Maya ceremonial center of some importance. Certain typical Classic features, such as temple-pyramids and hieroglyphic inscriptions, are lacking during its early development. Between the seventh and ninth centuries A.D., however, buildings were constructed with architectural features similar to those that appear in the Puuc area. But the only true example of the pure Puuc style is the Temple of the Three Lintels, which has fine veneer stonework. Other Classic Period structures, such as the Nunnery, the Akab-Dzib, the Casa Colorada, and the Iglesia, incorporate some elements of Puuc design, but they were all constructed with rough block masonry.

Also within the group of Maya Classic buildings stands the unusual round structure known as the Caracol. In its circular form, the building more closely resembles temples in central and eastern Mexico than it does any known Maya structure of the Classic Period. Nevertheless, its vaulted construction and architectural elements, particularly the continuous molding and the Chac mask, are definitely Mayan. An unclear inscription, questionably dated A.D. 909, is associated with the Caracol. Because the latest deciphered inscription of the Maya Classic Period at Chichén Itzá is dated A.D. 889, the combination of foreign design with native workmanship in the Caracol may indicate that this unusual structure dates from the period of cultural transition during which the Mexican or Mexican-allied foreigners were in the process of firmly establishing themselves at Chichén Itzá.

Radiocarbon dates associated with Mexican-style ceramics found at the sacred cave of Balankanche, near Chichén Itzá, indicate that Mexican influence was definitely being felt by the northern Maya by around the end of the ninth century. The beginning of Mexican dominance at Chichén Itzá is said by the native chronicles to have occurred within Katun 4 Ahau, the twenty-year period between A.D. 968 and 987. The architectural forms and cultural motifs that resulted from the three hundred years of intense activity during Chichén's Mexican Period show a striking resemblance to those known at the Toltec capital of Tula, fifty miles northwest of Mexico City. Although this similarity could have resulted from direct cultural contact between the two sites, it is more likely that Mexican influence initially spread to Yucatán through indirect channels. The aggressive Itzá, suggested by J. Eric Thompson to have been a Mexicanized group of the seafaring Putún Maya who controlled the trade routes around Yucatán, may well have been the vehicle for the instrusion of Mexican culture into Yucatán.

The Postclassic development of Chichén Itzá was clearly dominated by the aggressive foreigners, but the architecture and low-relief sculpture of northern Chichén show considerable evidence of a hybrid Mexican-Maya culture. Sculptural depictions of Maya priests and warriors attest to participation by the native Maya in ceremonial ritual and warfare, and it is clear that the Mexican-style architecture and sculpture were executed by native craftsmen employing their traditional stoneworking techniques. In addition, Maya religious traditions seem to have been publicly acknowledged by the foreigners for some time, for the traditional Chac mask of the northern Maya appears as a prominent decorative motif on the facades of such thoroughly Mexican structures as the Temple of the Warriors and the Castillo.

The Castillo is an unusual development of the temple-pyramid form and is one of the most striking accomplishments of Chichén's hybrid culture. It is believed to have been dedicated to Kukulcán, the Maya version of Quetzalcoatl, the feathered serpent god of central Mexico, shortly after the leader that assumed the name of Quetzalcoatl firmly established Mexican rule at Chichén Itzá. Set against the vast open space of the northern plaza, this pyramid, 180 feet wide and 75 feet high, has a striking visual and emotional effect. As well as creating an imposing appearance, the design of the pyramid symbolizes, by the numbers of its different architectural elements, the 365 days and eighteen months of the Maya year and the fifty-two years in the repeating year cycle known as the Calendar Round. Four wide stairways literally root the pyramid to the ground, and make the doorway openings of the temple building seem inviting and accessible, perhaps suggesting a more public use of the temple-pyramid than was characteristic of those built by the Classic Maya.

The Castillo stands at the center of northern Chichén, but it was the Sacred Cenote, several hundred yards farther north, that gave Chichén Itzá its renown as a pilgrimage site. The tradition of offering human sacrifice and valuable possessions to the rain gods thought to live in the cenote has been known since the Spanish Conquest. Bishop Landa wrote in the sixteenth century that "into this well it was their custom to cast living men as sacrifice to the gods in times of drought, and it was their belief that they did not die, although they never saw them anymore. They also threw in many other things of precious stone and articles which they highly prized."

When the cenote cult began is not known. Its presence at Chichén Itzá may well have been one reason why the Mexican intruders established themselves there. Some human sacrifice is definitely known to have been practiced at Maya ceremonial centers during the Classic Period, but, judging from such gruesome innovations as the Tzompantli, or skull rack, of northern Chichén, it is clear that human sacrifice became increasingly important during the Postclassic Period and was not necessarily limited to the cenote cult.

In addition to the militaristic processions and ceremonial rituals that must have taken place in northern Chichén, Bishop Landa mentions that a kind of outdoor public theater performance was presented on low "dance" platforms. Certainly too, multitudes of people must have thronged to watch the ritualistic competition of the ball game, which was apparently both a diversion and a brutal, mythological enactment of a religious cult, again involving human sacrifice. This ritual game must have been of supreme importance at Chichén Itzá, for in addition to the massive Great Court of northern Chichén, eight other such ball courts are known at the site.

Chichén Itzá apparently suffered a gradual cultural decline during the early thirteenth century, when Mexican leaders relocated their capital at the walled city of Mayapán. Chichén Itzá was not completely abandoned at this time, but there is little evidence of any significant construction at the site after A.D. 1200, and many of the buildings soon began to fall into ruin. Nevertheless, Chichén Itzá remained a great pilgrimage site, and the sacrificial cult at the Sacred Cenote apparently reached its peak after the close of the Mexican Period, even continuing on into Colonial times.

The final occupation of Chichén Itzá ultimately brings us back to the confused history of the legendary Itzá, who throughout their occupation of Yucatán were apparently never accepted by the native Maya. Some historical accounts indicate that the majority of the Itzá were driven from Chichén Itzá around A.D. 1200, although a different interpretation of the chronicles places their expulsion some 250 years later, just before the fall of Mayapán. Though the chronology may vary, it is known that upon leaving northern Yucatán the enigmatic Itzá made an important final migration in which they withdrew into the rain forest of the Petén and settled at the lake named for them—Petén Itzá. There, on their isolated island stronghold of Tayasal, they remained one of the last unconquered Maya kingdoms, and were finally overwhelmed by the Spanish only in 1697, more than 150 years after the actual conquest of Yucatán.

65. *The massive Nunnery, like all but one of Chichén Itzá's Classic Period structures, was built with the rough block wall and slab vault masonry techniques inherited from the southern lowlands. Several different stages of this type of construction can be seen at the building's northeast end.*

66. The Nunnery Annex is a late addition to the main building. The entire facade of the Annex's east end is decorated in a manner somewhat reminiscent of the Chenes style, but the overall design of the open-mouthed serpent mask seems to have been less important than the clear representation of separate decorative motifs.

67. *Just a few feet from the Nunnery Annex stands the Iglesia, or church, a thick-walled temple of only one room. A roof comb rises directly above its west wall in the form of a flying facade, giving the front of the small structure the appearance of considerable height.*

68. The fully reconstructed Temple of the Three Lintels shows both the architectural design and the fine veneer masonry stonework typical of the pure Puuc style. The inscriptions carved on the stone lintels are indecipherable, but it is thought the temple dates from around A.D. 875.

69. The Caracol is named for the snail-like, spiral form of its interior stairway. The careful orientation of the narrow sight openings in the small room at the top of the forty-foot structure indicates that the Caracol was probably designed to serve as an observatory as well as a temple or watchtower.

70. The Casa Colorada, or red house, is set upon a platform to the west of the Caracol. Like the Iglesia, it has a flying facade. A second, taller roof comb once stood behind the flying facade.

71. The Castillo, dating from the Mexican occupation of Chichén Itzá, was dedicated to the cult of Kukulcán, the deified culture hero of central Mexico whose symbol was the feathered serpent. The Temple of the Warriors is also a Mexican building, thought to have been dedicated to the Mexican cult of war.

72. *The upper Temple of the Jaguars stands atop the thirty-foot east wall of the Ball Court. The temple, with a Mexican design, is named for the line of jaguars, the symbol of a Mexican military order, that decorates its lower frieze area.*

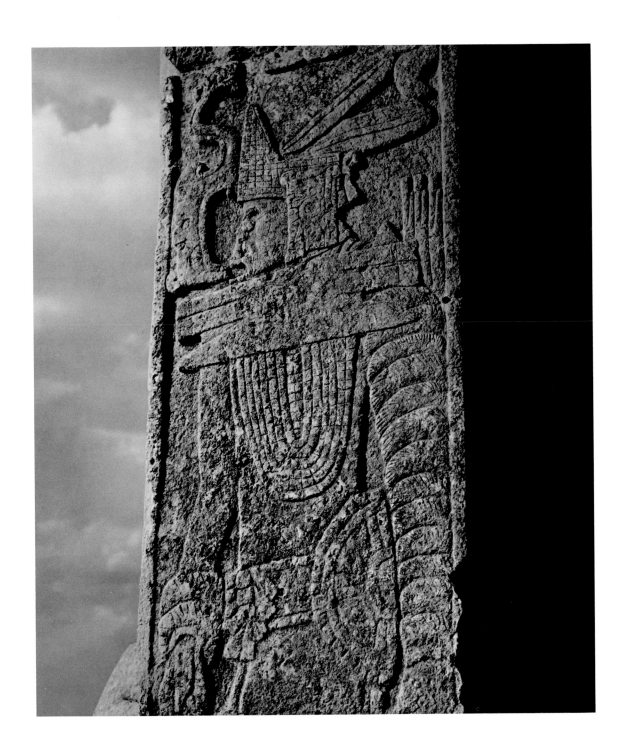

73. A typical Mexican warrior is depicted on the square portico columns of the upper Temple of the Jaguars. His characterization and style of dress are unmistakably Mexican, but the fine low-relief carving was probably done by a native Maya sculptor.

XII. Tulum

We followed the shore day and night, and the next day toward sunset we perceived a city or town so large, that Seville would not have seemed more considerable nor better; one saw there a very large tower; on the shore was a great throng of Indians, who bore two standards which they raised and lowered to signal us to approach them; the commander [Grijalva] did not wish it. The same day we came to a beach near which was the highest tower we had seen. . . .

Juan de Grijalva expedition, 1518
In Sylvanus G. Morley, *The Ancient Maya*, p. 102

It is likely that the coastal town which Grijalva's expedition sighted in 1518 was Tulum. The site is known to have been inhabited during the sixteenth century, and Tulum's Castillo, standing on a cliff thirty-five feet above the Caribbean, would have looked like a tower from the sea. Like Mayapán, the walled city that replaced Chichén Itzá as the Postclassic capital of Yucatán, Tulum was a residential settlement that reached its peak of development between A.D. 1200 and 1450. The two contemporaneous sites—Mayapán and Tulum—differ significantly in size and layout, but they were both fortified urban settlements protected by defensive walls. The enclosed area of Tulum is only some 450 yards long by about 200 yards wide. The town was probably never inhabited by more than about five hundred persons. The walls of Mayapán, on the other hand, enclosed an area of four square kilometers, into which some two thousand dwellings and over ten thousand persons were crowded.

In its overall plan, Tulum resembled a typical highland Mexican town. A main street running north and south served as the central axis for civic and residential buildings. The principal temples, the Castillo and the Temple of the Frescoes, had a combination of Mexican and Maya features, though most of Tulum's buildings were residential structures built with the rough block masonry and flat beam and mortar roofs used throughout the east coast of Yucatán even during Classic times. Tulum's buildings were more solidly built than Mayapán's, even though archaeological evidence shows that Tulum was not occupied before the eleventh century and probably postdates the initial settlement of Mayapán. The buildings of both sites were coated with heavy layers of plaster to give a smooth final coating over the rough block masonry construction. Some of Tulum's stucco decoration still remains on its sturdy, simple structures, and even parts of its distinctive fresco paintings are still visible on some temple walls.

Although certain unmistakable elements of Mexican culture appear at Tulum, the east coast of Yucatán remained comparatively isolated even during the Postclassic Period, and continued the independent cultural development that characterized it during the Classic Period. Archaeological evidence at the great site of Cobá and as far south as British Honduras indicates that a simple, homogeneous native culture continued to exist along most of the east coast during the thirteenth and fourteenth centuries. Nevertheless, as the thick, defensive walls protecting Tulum clearly indicate, the impact of the competitive warfare and repressive tyranny with which Mayapán's rulers controlled northern Yucatán was strongly felt even on the east coast. The actual bloodlines of the Mexican intruders may have been absorbed by Yucatán's resilient native population within a few centuries, but the aggressive militarism introduced by the foreigners endured well after the close of the Mexican Period.

Mayapán's tyrannical domination of Yucatán was finally ended around 1450, and the walled city was sacked and abandoned. But the sixteen independent Maya tribes then withdrew to their separate states only to engage in constant, bitter warfare over political control of the peninsula. Their irreconcilable enmities unquestionably contributed to the success of the Spanish Conquest, and their tragic insecurity in the midst of dissolving cultural traditions was intensified in the last half of the fifteenth century by natural calamities over which they had no control. Native accounts recorded by Bishop Landa indicate that the peninsula was leveled in 1464 by a devastating hurricane and that in 1480 a widespread plague struck the people. In 1514, just three years after a few shipwrecked Spaniards were taken captive by the northern Maya, a terrible epidemic of smallpox broke out, beginning the decimation of the native population by disease that eventually ravaged the entire lowland area.

The warring northern Maya successfully resisted conquest by the Spanish until 1541. Although most of Yucatán's ceremonial centers were abandoned by the time of the Conquest, sites as isolated as Cobá and Tulum continued to be occupied until at least the end of the sixteenth century. Ceramic ware of the Colonial Period indicates continued activity at Tulum until around 1618, one hundred years after the site was apparently sighted by Grijalva. Throughout the Colonial Period, Tulum was often used as a defensive stronghold by eastern Maya rebelling against Spanish authorities. Even in the first quarter of the twentieth century, few outsiders dared make prolonged visits to the site because of the hostile natives.

In recent years, however, with the opening up of Yucatán's east coast and the clearing and preservation of Tulum, the appearance of the site has changed dramatically. There is little talk now of the dwarf people who the local natives believed inhabited the small, low-doored structures. We are most struck today by the natural setting of Tulum, by the site's exhilarating sense of standing on the edge of unlimited oceanic space.

But Tulum is also infused with a certain sadness, for the few buildings dominating the bare, windswept site are in reality crude, clumsy structures, ones which awaken in us little of the awe or sense of grandeur evoked by the great achievements of the Classic Period. Standing with its back to the sea, Tulum provides enduring evidence of the will of a people, but at the same time, like the prophetic warning chant recorded in *The Book of the Chilam Balam of Tizimin,* its physical presence is in itself a moving expression of the end of a world, an epilogue to a culture:

> Eat, eat, thou hast bread;
> Drink, drink, thou hast water;
> On that day, dust possesses the earth,
> On that day, a blight is on the face of the earth,
> On that day, a cloud rises,
> On that day, a strong man seizes the land,
> On that day, things fall to ruin,
> On that day, the tender leaf is destroyed,
> On that day, three signs are on the tree,
> On that day, three generations hang there,
> On that day, the battle flag is raised,
> And they are scattered afar in the forests.

> *The Maya Chronicles*
> Translated by D. G. Brinton

110

74. *The view south along the coast at Tulum shows Structure 45 on the left; the Castillo, behind it, standing with its back to the sea; and the diminutive Temple of the Diving God on the right. Submerged coral reefs and a rough coast effectively protected the small town on its eastern side.*

75. Still in place above the doorway of the Temple of the Diving
God is the peculiar, upside-down stucco figure for which the small
temple is named. This unusual mythological motif, perhaps of
non-Maya origin, is a prominent decorative element on many of
Tulum's buildings.

76. *The Caribbean Sea from the northern end of Tulum.*

Bibliography

Books

Blom, Frans. *The Conquest of Yucatán.* New York: 1936.

——, and Gertrude Duby Blom. *La selva lacandona.* 2 vols. Mexico City: 1955-57.

Bolles, T. *La Iglesia.* San Francisco: 1963.

Brinton, D. G.*The Maya Chronicles.* Philadelphia: 1882.

Catherwood, Frederick. *Views of Ancient Monuments in Central America, Chiapas, and Yucatán.* New York: 1844.

Charlot, Jean. *An Artist on Art.* Honolulu: 1972.

Charnay, Desiré. *Ancient Cities of the New World.* London: 1887.

Coe, Michael . *The Maya.* New York: 1966.

Coe, William R. *Tikal: A Handbook of the Ancient Maya Ruins.* Philadelphia: 1969.

Covarrubias, Miguel. *Indian Art of Mexico and Central America.* New York: 1957

Culbert, T. Patrick, ed. *The Classic Maya Collapse.* Albuquerque, N.M.: 1973.

de la Fuente, Beatriz. *La escultura de Palenque.* Mexico City: 1965.

—— . *Palenque en la historia y en el arte.* Mexico City: 1968.

Deuel, Leo. *Conquistadores without Swords: Archaeologists in the Americas.* New York: 1967.

Foncerrada de Molina, Marta. *La escultura arquitectónica de Uxmal.* Mexico City: 1965.

——. *Uxmal: la ciudad del dios de la lluvia.* Mexico City: 1968.

Gallenkamp, Charles. *Maya: The Riddle and Rediscovery of a Lost Civilization.* New York: 1962.

Gates, William, ed. *Yucatán, Before and After the Conquest.* Baltimore: 1937.

Gilpin, Laura. *Temples in Yucatán: A Camera Chronicle of Chichén Itzá.* New York: 1948.

Gordon, G. B. *Prehistoric Ruins of Copán, Honduras.* Memoirs of the Peabody Museum of Archaeology and Ethnology, vol. 1, no. 1. Cambridge, Mass.: 1896.

Graham, Ian. *The Art of Maya Hieroglyphic Writing.* Catalogue for exhibit sponsored by Peabody Museum of Archaeology and Ethnology and Center for InterAmerican Relations, Inc. Cambridge, Mass.: 1971.

Graham, John A., ed. *Ancient Mesoamerica, Selected Readings.* Palo Alto, Calif.: 1966.

Greene, Merle. *Ancient Maya Relief Sculpture.* Museum of Primitive Art. New York: 1967.

Halle, Louis J., Jr. *River of Ruins.* New York: 1941.

Hyams, Edward. *Soil and Civilisation.* London: 1952.

Kelemen, Pal. *Medieval American Art.* 2 vols. 3rd ed. New York: 1969.

Kubler, George. *Art and Architecture of Ancient America.* Baltimore: 1962.

——. *The Shape of Time: Remarks on the History of Things.* New Haven, Conn.: 1965.

Lothrop, S. K. *Tulum: An Archaeological Study of the East Coast of Yucatán.* Carnegie Institution of Washington, Publication 335. Washington, D.C.: 1924.

Maler, Teobert. *Explorations in the Department of Petén, Guatemala.* Memoirs of the Peabody Museum of Archaeology and Ethnology, vol. 5, no. 1. Cambridge, Mass.: 1911.

——. *Researches in the Central Portion of the Usumacinta Valley.* Memoirs of the Peabody Museum of Archaeology and Ethnology, vol. 2, nos. 1 and 2. Cambridge, Mass.: 1901, 1903.

Marquina, Ignacio. *Arquitectura prehispánica.* Mexico City: 1951.

Maudslay, A. C., and A. P. Maudslay. *A Glimpse at Guatemala.* London: 1899.

Maudslay, A. P. *Biología centrali-americana, archaeology.* 4 vols. plates, 1 vol. text. London: 1889–1902.

Morley, Sylvanus G. *The Ancient Maya.* 3rd ed., rev. by George W. Brainerd. Stanford, Calif.: 1956.

——. *Guidebook to the Ruins of Quiriguá.* Carnegie Institution of Washington, Supplementary Publication 16. Washington, D.C.: 1935.

Olsen, Charles. *Mayan Letters.* Cape editions 17. London: 1968.

Price, Christine. *Heirs of the Ancient Maya.* Photographs by Gertrude Duby Blom. New York: 1972.

Proskouriakoff, Tatiana. *An Album of Maya Architecture.* Norman, Okla.: 1963.

——. *Study of Classic Maya Sculpture.* Carnegie Institution of Washington. Publication 593. Washington, D.C.: 1950.

Recinos, Adrian. *Popul Vuh; The Sacred Book of the Ancient Quiché Maya.* Norman, Okla.: 1950.

Roys, Ralph. *The Book of the Chilam Balam of Chumayel.* Norman, Okla.: 1967.

Ruppert, K. *The Caracol at Chichén Itzá, Yucatán.* Carnegie Institution of Washington, Publication 543. Washington, D.C.: 1935.

——, J. Eric Thompson, and Tatiana Proskouriakoff. *Bonampak, Chiapas, Mexico.* Carnegie Institution of Washington, Publication 602. Washington, D.C.: 1955.

Ruz Lhuiller, Alberto. *Chichén Itzá: Official Guide.* Mexico City: 1967.

———. *La civilización de los antiguos mayas.* Mexico City: 1963.

———. *Palenque: Official Guide.* Mexico City: 1960.

———. *Uxmal: Official Guide.* Mexico City: 1967.

Sanders, W. T. *Prehistoric Ceramics and Settlement Patterns in Quintana Roo, Mexico.* Carnegie Institution of Washington, Publication 613. Washington, D.C.: 1957.

———, and B. J. Price. *Mesoamerica: The Evolution of a Civilization.* New York: 1968.

Spinden, Herbert J. *Maya Art and Civilization.* Indian Hills, Colo.: 1957.

Stephens, J. L. *Incidents of Travel in Central America, Chiapas and Yucatán.* 2 vols. 1841; reprints New Brunswick, N.J.: 1949; New York: 1969.

———. *Incidents of Travel in Yucatán.* 2 vols. 1843; reprint New York: 1963.

Stierlin, Henri. *Mayan Architecture.* New York: 1964.

Stromsvik, Gustav. *Guide Book to the Ruins of Copán.* Carnegie Institution of Washington, Publication 577. Washington, D.C.: 1947.

Thompson, J. Eric. *Maya Archaeologist.* London: 1963.

———. *Maya Hieroglyphic Writing: An Introduction.* Norman, Okla.: 1960.

———. *Maya History and Religion.* Norman, Okla.: 1971.

———. *The Rise and Fall of Maya Civilization.* Norman, Okla.: 1954.

———, H. E. D. Pollock, and J. Charlot. *A Preliminary Study of the Ruins of Cobá, Quintana Roo, Mexico.* Carnegie Institution of Washington, Publication 424. Washington, D.C.: 1932.

Tozzer, A. M. *Chichén Itzá and Its Cenote of Sacrifice.* Memoirs of the Peabody Museum of Archaeology and Ethnology, vols. 11, 12. Cambridge, Mass.: 1957.

———, ed. *Landa's Relación de las Cosas Yucatán.* Papers of the Peabody Museum of Archaeology and Ethnology, vol. 18. Cambridge, Mass.: 1941.

Tulum: Official Guide. Mexico City: 1961.

Vogt, E. Z., and Alberto Ruz Lhuiller. *Desarrollo cultural de los Mayas.* Mexico City: 1964.

Von Hagen, Victor. *Frederick Catherwood, Architect.* New York: 1950.

———. *Maya Explorer.* Norman, Okla.: 1947.

———. *Maya: Land of the Turkey and the Deer.* New York: 1960

Wauchope, Robert. *They Found the Buried Cities.* Chicago: 1965.

———, ed. *Handbook of Middle American Indians.* Vol. II. *Archaeology of Southern Mesoamerica.* Gordon R. Willey, vol. ed. Austin, Tex.: 1965.

Westheim, Paul *The Art of Ancient Mexico.* New York: 1965.

———. *Ideas fundamentales del arte prehispánico.* Mexico City: 1959.

———. *The Sculpture of Ancient Mexico.* New York: 1963.

Wolf, Eric R. *Sons of the Shaking Earth.* Chicago: 1959.

Articles

Adams, Richard E. W. "Suggested Classic Period Occupational Specialization in the Southern Maya Lowlands." *Monographs and Papers in Maya Archaeology,* W. R. Bullard, ed. Papers of the Peabody Museum of Archaeology and Ethnology, vol. 61, no. 2. Cambridge, Mass.: 1970.

Andrews, E. Wyllys IV. "Excavations at Dzibilchaltún, Northwestern Yucatán, Mexico." *Proceedings of the American Philosophical Society,* vol. 104, no. 3 (1960).

———. "Dzibilchaltún, a Northern Maya Metropolis." *Archaeology,* vol. 21, no. 1 (1968).

Berlin, H. "A Critique of Dates at Palenque." *American Antiquity,* vol. 10, no. 4 (1945).

Blom, Frans. "Yaxchilán, la ciudad maravillosa de los mayas." Unpublished MS.

Borhegyi, Stephen F. "America's Ballgame." *Natural History,* vol. 69, no. 1 (1960).

Coe, Michael D. "The Funerary Temple among the Classic Maya." *Southwestern Journal of Anthropology,* vol. 21, no. 2 (1956).

———. "A Model of Ancient Community Structure in the Maya Lowlands." *Southwestern Journal of Anthropology,* vol. 21, no. 2 (1965).

Coe, William R. "Tikal, Guatemala, and Emergent Maya Civilization." *Science,* vol. 147, no. 3664 (1965).

———. "Tikal: Ten Years of Study of a Maya Ruin in the Lowlands of Guatemala." *Expedition,* vol. 8, no. 1 (1965).

Harrison, Peter D. "Form and Function in a Maya 'Palace' Group." *International Congress of Americanists,* 38 sess., vol. 1 (1968).

Haviland, William S. "Ancient Lowland Maya Social Organization." *Archaeological Studies in Middle America.* Middle American Research Institute, Tulane University, Publication 26 (1968).

———. "A New Population Estimate for Tikal, Guatemala." *American Antiquity,* vol. 34, no. 4 (1969).

———. "Stature at Tikal, Guatemala: Implications for Ancient Maya Demography and Social Organization." *American Antiquity,* vol. 32, no. 3 (1967).

———. "Tikal, Guatemala and Mesoamerican Urbanism." *World Archaeology,* vol. 2, no. 2 (1970)

Kelley, David H. "Glyphic Evidence for a Dynastic Sequence at Quiriguá, Guatemala." *American Antiquity,* vol. 27, no. 3 (1962).

Kubler, George. "Studies in Classic Maya Iconography." *Memoirs of Connecticut Academy of Arts and Sciences,* vol. 18 (1969).

Proskouriakoff, Tatiana. "Historical Data in the Inscriptions of Yaxchilán." *Estudios de cultura maya,* vols 3 and 4 (1963, 1964).

———. "Historical Implications of a Pattern of Dates at Piedras Negras, Guatemala. " *American Antiquity,* vol. 25, no. 4 (1960).

———. "The Lords of the Maya Realm." *Expedition,* vol. 4, no. 1 (1961).

———. "Mayapán, the Last Stronghold of a Civilization." *Archaeology,* vol. 7, no. 2 (1954).

———. "Portraits of Women in Maya Art." In *Essays in Pre-Columbian Art and Archaeology,* S. K. Lothrop, ed. Cambridge, Mass.: 1961.

Puleston, Dennis E., and Olga S. Puleston. "An Ecological Approach to the Origins of Maya Civilization." *Archaeology,* vol. 24, no. 4 (1971).

Rands, Robert L., and Barbara C. Rands. "The Ceramic Position of Palenque, Chiapas." *American Antiquity,* vol. 23, no. 2 (1957).

Ruz Lhuiller, Alberto. "The Mystery of the Temple of the Inscriptions." *Archaeology,* vol. 6 (March 1953).

———. "The Pyramid Tomb of a Prince of Palenque." *The Illustrated London News* (August 29, 1953). Reprinted in *Conquistadores without Swords,* L. Deuel, ed.

Sabloff, Jeremy, and Gordon R. Willey. "The Collapse of Maya Civilization in the Southern Lowlands: A Consideration of History and Process." *Southwestern Journal of Anthropology,* vol. 23, no. 4 (1967).

Sanders, William T. "Cultural Ecology of the Maya Lowlands." *Estudios de cultura maya,* vols. 2 and 3 (1962, 1963).

Thompson, J. Eric. "A Trial Survey of the Northern Maya Area." *American Antiquity,* vol. 11, no. 1 (1945).

Villa Rojas, Alfonso. "The Yaxuná-Cobá Causeway." *Contributions to American Archaeology,* vol. 2, no. 9 (1934).

Willey, Gordon R. "The Structure of Ancient Maya Society: Evidence from the Southern Lowlands." *American Anthropologist,* vol. 58, no. 5 (1956).

Index

NOTE: Page numbers on which an entry is illustrated are in italics.

Acropolis (Copán), 19, *27*
Akab-Dzib (Chichén Itzá), 95
Album of Maya Architecture, An (Proskouriakoff), 72
Ancient Maya, The (Morley), 108
Andrews, E. Wyllys, IV, 68

Ball Court (Chichén Itzá), *106*
Ball Court (Copán), 16, *20*, *21*
Bird Jaguar, 41, *45*, *46*, *47*
Blom, Frans, 39, 42
Blom, Gertrude Duby, 42
Bonampak, 41, 52, *53–54*
Book of the Chilam Balam of Chumayel, The (Roys, trans.), 94
Book of the Chilam Balam of Tizimin, The, 110
Brinton, D. G., 110
British Honduras, 109
British Museum, 40

Caracol (Chichén Itzá), 95, *103*, *104*
Caribbean Sea, *113*
Casa Colorada (Chichén Itzá), 95, *104*
Castillo (Chichén Itzá), 96, *105*
Castillo (Tulum), 108, *111*
Chac masks, 72, 73, *78*, *79*, 83, 96
Chichén Itzá, 70, 73, 74, 83, *94–97*, *99–107*
    Akab-Dzib, 95
    Ball Court, *106*
    Caracol, 95, *103*, *104*
    Casa Colorada, 95, *104*
    Castillo, 96, *105*
    Great Court, 97
    Iglesia, 95, *101*, 104
    Nunnery, 95, *99*, *100*, 101
    Sacred Cenote, 95, 96, 97
    Temple of the Jaguars, *106*, *107*
    Temple of the Three Lintels, 95, *102*
    Temple of the Warriors, 96, *105*
Cobá, 70, *71*, 109
    El Rey, 70
    Nohoch-Mul, 70, *71*
Codz-Poop (Puuc), 73, *78*, *79*
Coe, Michael, 70
Conquistadores without Swords (Deuel), 57
Copán, 15–18, *19–35*, 36, 56
    Acropolis, 19, *27*
    Ball Court, 16, *20*, *21*
    Court of the Hieroglyphic Stairway, *20*, *33*
    Great Plaza, *26*, *30*
    Hieroglyphic Court, *24*
    Reviewing Stand, *22*
    West Court, *22*, *23*, *27*
Copán River, 36
Court of the Hieroglyphic Stairway (Copán), *20*, *33*

Dove group (Uxmal), 82, *87*
Dzibilchaltún, 67–68, *69*, 82
    Temple of the Seven Dolls, 69

Edzná (Puuc), 72, 73, *75*
El Rey (Cobá), 70
Explorations in the Department of Petén, Guatemala (Maler), 1

Governor's Palace (Uxmal), 80, 82, 83, *91*, *92*
Great Court (Chichén Itzá), 97
Great Plaza (Copán), *26*, *30*
Great Plaza (Tikal), 2, 4, *5*, *6*
Grijalva, Juan de, 108, 109

Hachakyum, 41
Halle, Louis J., Jr., 55
Handbook of Middle American Indians (Wauchope, ed.), 4n
Hieroglyphic Court (Copán), *24*
House of the Turtles (Uxmal), *93*

Iglesia (Chichén Itzá), 95, *101*, 104
Incidents of Travel in Central America, Chiapas and Yucatán (Stephens), 15, 36, 58, 80–82
Itzá. *See* Chichén Itzá

Jaguar clan (Yaxchilán), 40–41
    See also Bird Jaguar; Shield Jaguar
Jaguars, Temple of (Chichén Itzá), *106*, *107*

Kabáh (Puuc), 72, 73, 74, *78*
Kukulcán, 96, *105*

Labná (Puuc), 72, 73, *77*
Lacandón Maya, 41, 52
Lacanhá River, 52

Lake Cobá, 70
Lake Macanxoc, 70
Landa, Bishop, 67, 96, 97, 109

Machu Picchu, 58
Maler, Teobert, 1, 40
Mausdlay, Alfred, 40
Maya, The (Coe), 70
Maya Chronicles, The (Brinton), 110
Mayapán, 97, 108
Mérida, 68, 95
Mexico City, 40, 96
Morley, Sylvanus G., 108
Motagua River, 36

National Museum of Anthropology (Mexico City),
   40, 42
Nohoch-Mul (Cobá), 70, 71
North Acropolis (Tikal), 2
North Terrace (Tikal), 2
Nunnery (Chichén Itzá), 95, 99, 100, 101
Nunnery Quadrangle (Uxmal), 80, 82, 83, 88, 89, 90

Palace Complex (Palenque), 59, 60
Palenque, 17, 40, 55–58, 59–66
   Palace Complex, 59, 60
   Royal Tomb, 57
   Temple of the Cross, 56
   Temple of the Foliated Cross, 56, 63
   Temple of the Inscriptions, 56, 57, 59, 61
   Temple of the Sun, 56, 62, 63
Palomas group (Uxmal), 82, 87
Peru, 58
Petén, 1, 2, 40, 67, 70, 72, 82, 97
Petén Itzá, 97
Piedras Negras, 40, 52, 56
Proskouriakoff, Tatiana, 40, 41, 52, 72
Putún Maya, 96
Puuc, 72–74, 75–79, 80–83, 85–93
   Codz-Poop, 73, 78, 79
   Edzná, 72, 73, 75
   Kabáh, 72, 73, 74, 78
   Labná, 72, 73, 77
   Sayil, 72, 73, 76
   Uxmal, 72, 73, 74, 80–83, 85–93
Pyramid of the Magician (Uxmal), 80–82, 85, 86, 88

Quetzalcoatl, 96
Quintana Roo, 70
Quiriguá, 16, 36, 37–38

Reviewing Stand (Copán), 22
River of Ruins (Halle), 55
Royal Tomb (Palenque), 57
Roys, Ralph, 94
Ruz Lhuiller, Alberto, 57

Sacred Cenote (Chichén Itzá), 95, 96, 97
Sayil (Puuc), 72, 73, 76
Shield Jaguar, 41, 46, 48
Spinden, Herbert, 17
Stephens, John L., 15, 36, 58, 80–82, 87

Tajín culture, 56
Tayasal, 97
Temple of the Cross (Palenque), 56
Temple of the Diving God (Tulum), 111, 112
Temple of the Foliated Cross (Palenque), 56, 63
Temple of the Frescoes (Tulum), 108
Temple of the Inscriptions (Palenque), 56, 57, 59, 61
Temple of the Jaguars (Chichén Itzá), 106, 107
Temple of the Seven Dolls (Dzibilchaltún), 69
Temple of the Sun (Palenque), 56, 62, 63
Temple of the Three Lintels (Chichén Itzá), 95, 102
Temple of the Warriors (Chichén Itzá), 96, 105
Teotihuacán, 3
Thompson, J. Eric, 4, 52, 96
Tikal, 1–4, 5–14, 68
   Great Plaza, 2, 4, 5, 6
   North Acropolis, 2
   North Terrace, 2
   Twin-Pyramid Complexes, 9, 10
Tlaloc, 82
Totonac culture, 56
Tula, 96
Tulum, 71, 108–10, 111–13
   Castillo, 108, 111
   Temple of the Diving God, 111, 112
   Temple of the Frescoes, 108
Twin-Pyramid Complexes (Tikal), 9, 10

Usumacinta River, 40, 41, 42, 45, 56
Uxmal, 72, 73, 74, 80–83, 85–93
   Governor's Palace, 80, 82, 83, 91, 92
   House of the Turtles, 93
   Nunnery Quadrangle, 80, 82, 83, 88, 89, 90
   Palomas group, 82, 87
   Pyramid of the Magician, 80–82, 85, 86, 88

Veracruz, 56
Villa Rojas, Alfonso, 80

West Court (Copán), 22, 23, 27
Westheim, Paul, 17

Yaxchilán, 17, 39–42, 43–51, 52
"Yaxchilán, la ciudad maravillosa de los Mayas"
   (Blom), 39
Yaxuná, 70
"Yaxuná-Cobá Causeway, The" (Villa Rojas), 80
Yucatán, 67, 70, 73, 76, 82, 97, 108, 109
Yucatán, Before and After the Conquest
   (Gates, ed.), 67

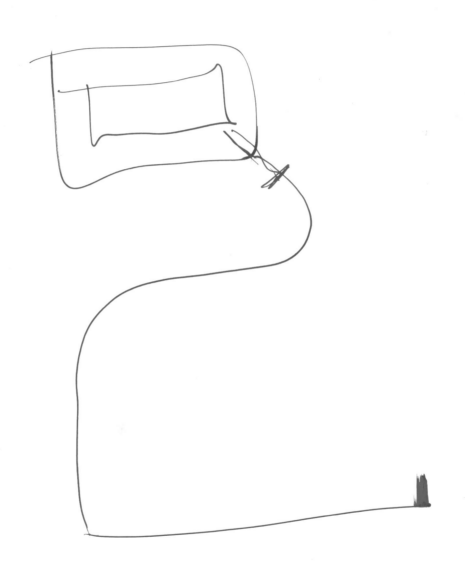